Glenbow Ranch Provincial Park

GRASS, HILLS, AND HISTORY

FRED STENSON

Kingsley
PUBLISHING

Published in Canada and the United States by Kingsley Publishing
www.kingsleypublishing.ca

Cover and interior design: John Luckhurst
Front cover image: Patrick Price

Every effort has been made to obtain permission to print the images in this book. The publisher would be pleased to adjust credits upon reprinting.

Printed in Canada by Friesens

2012/1
First Edition

Library and Archives Canada Cataloguing in Publication

Stenson, Fred, 1951-
Glenbow Ranch Provincial Park : grass, hills, and history /
Fred Stenson.

Includes bibliographical references and index.
ISBN 978-1-926832-14-2

1. Glenbow Ranch Provinical Park (Alta.)—Anecdotes.
2. Natural history—Glenbow Ranch Provincial Park (Alta.).
3. Native peoples—Glenbow Ranch Provincial Park (Alta.)—History.
4. Harvie, Eric Lafferty, 1892-1975—Family. I. Title.

FC3665.G54S74 2012   971.23'38   C2012-902320-5

Ordering information:
www.kingsleypublishing.ca
or
www.alpinebookpeddlers.ca

Premier of Alberta

Office of the Premier
Legislature Building
Edmonton, Alberta
Canada T5K 2B6
Telephone 780 427 2251
Fax 780 427 1349

Message from Honourable Alison Redford, QC
Premier of Alberta

On behalf of the Government of Alberta, it is my pleasure to congratulate the Glenbow Ranch Park Foundation on the publication of this book, telling the story of Glenbow Ranch Provincial Park and its place in our history.

Glenbow Ranch Provincial Park showcases Alberta's rich natural heritage and cultural history. It protects breathtaking landscapes, endangered ecosystems, important watershed and grasslands, and it tells the history of First Nations, early settlers, ranching and industrial development. Sandstone from the quarry was even used in the construction of the Alberta Legislature.

Our provincial parks offer Albertans and visitors access to some of the most spectacular natural landscapes, species and habitat in the world. These parks are integral to our quality of life, and they play a significant role in helping to make Alberta a great place to live and raise a family.

The Government of Alberta is proud to acknowledge the vision and generosity of the Eric Harvie family, in making it possible for this land to remain undeveloped and to serve as a legacy for all Albertans.

I know that Albertans, and visitors from across Canada and around the world will enjoy learning more about the unique aspects of Glenbow Ranch Provincial Park, and the legacy of conservation, education and recreational opportunities that this magnificent park offers.

Alison Redford, QC

2012

Freedom To Create. Spirit To Achieve.

Message from the Honourable Cindy Ady
Minister of Tourism, Parks and Recreation

Protecting more than 1300 hectares of spectacular landscape along the Bow River between Calgary and Cochrane, Glenbow Ranch Provincial Park provides a unique opportunity to celebrate Alberta's rich ranching history and culture.

The Government of Alberta recognized and valued the Harvie family's vision for their land, and their generous offer to sell the land below its assessed market value. The purchase was completed in August 2006, and the land designated as a provincial park.

Prior to opening the park to the public in August 2011, significant environmental and ecological assessments were done to ensure that this land would be managed appropriately in the years ahead. As managers and stewards of this provincial treasure, we are committed to ensuring that these landscapes and wildlife will be here for future generations to enjoy.

Albertans have a deep connection to the land. Nature has an important place in our hearts, minds and souls. As a province, we will continue to ensure that *"Alberta's parks inspire people to discover, value, protect, and enjoy the natural world and the benefits it provides for current and future generations."*

Together with the Glenbow Ranch Park Foundation, we are committed to ensuring an amazing experience for park visitors, as well as protecting and preserving the complex and fragile natural and historical resources in the park.

I invite you to read this book and spend some time connecting to this great park through education programs, outdoor recreation, or simply spending time in nature.

Cindy Ady
Minister of Alberta Tourism, Parks and Recreation

Alberta

229 Legislature Building, Edmonton, Alberta T5K 2B6 Canada Telephone 780-427-4928 Fax 780-427-0188
#328, 22 Midlake Blvd. SE, Calgary, Alberta T2X 2X7 Canada Telephone 403-256-8969 Fax 403-256-8970

Printed on recycled paper

Contents

Preface

OUR FAMILY HAS BEEN RANCHING IN THE BOW River Valley for over seventy years. We do so because we love the life, the business, and the land itself. Now, the bond we have with the land has led us to part with it, so it can become an Alberta provincial park. As a provincial park, the land will be protected for all time. It will remain a grassland and become even more natural and beautiful as time goes by.

> The idea of turning the ranch into a protected park has been in our family for a long time.

The idea of turning the ranch into a protected park has been in our family for a long time. It was seeded in the minds of my sisters and myself by our late father, Neil Harvie. When acreage development was spreading in our direction from Calgary in the 1970s, I remember asking my father what would happen to our ranch. I asked if it would become developed too. I clearly remember his answer. He said that the ranch would make a heck of a good park for public enjoyment. He also predicted that there would come a time when the public would put equal or greater value on open space and environmental protection than it did on housing development, *especially* in the vicinity of big cities. Said over thirty years ago, his predictions have come true.

Each of the last three generations of the Harvie family has played a role in making this park a reality. Our grand-

parents, Eric and Dorothy Harvie, recognized the beauty of the property and bought it. Our father, Neil Harvie, saw both the land's beauty and the threat posed to it by development. It was left to my sisters and me to go beyond recognition of beauty and threat and take action to preserve the ranch for the future.

The choice of how to achieve this goal was again guided by our father, who financed research into government rules for land donation. The resulting changes to the law made it possible and practical for my sisters and me to offer the land to the provincial government as a park in exchange for cash and a tax receipt. The changed rules allowed us to do what we really wanted, which was to protect the land and allow others to enjoy it as we had. As for timing, my personal wish was to do it as soon as possible so that I could see it go from working ranch to park in

Glenbow Ranch Provincial Park: an extraordinary work of conservation on the surging fringe of a major city.

my lifetime. My sisters and I also understood that our family has a role to play in the maintenance and improvement of the park, and so we created the Harvie Conservancy Fund. The money is to be used to support improvements to Glenbow Ranch Provincial Park.

I will admit there are times when I look across the valley from my ranch house at what is now Glenbow Ranch Provincial Park and think what a delight it was to own and ranch that beautiful place. What I do in such moments is remind myself that we are only on this earth for a short time and that, because of the creation of the park, it will look the same, natural and beautiful, long after I am gone.

There was one more idea behind the surrender of the ranch and that was the hope that our action might inspire others in like positions to make similar land donations. From the vantage of the present, Alberta's and Canada's future can be greatly improved by the preservation of such islands of peace and beauty. To all future visitors to Glenbow Ranch Provincial Park, my wish is this: that you feast your mind and senses, and enjoy.

Yours truly,
Tim Harvie

Introduction

Right: An abandoned cable wheel is a memory of Glenbow's industrial age.

The line of spruce trees visible behind the remains of a general store marks the Bow River: the dividing line between what is conserved and what is farmed or otherwise developed in the Bow River Valley.

CONSIDER WHAT A PARK IS. A PLACE REMOVED from the wheel of development; a place restored to nature and the forces of nature; a place with all its historical markings intact, while the land and structures around it continue to obey the briefer cycles of market and economy.

Glenbow Ranch Provincial Park was legislated into existence by the Province of Alberta in August 2006. As with any transition, the actual day is a milestone rather than a beginning or an end. The storyline of this landscape as a park perhaps began in 1929 with the stock market collapse and ensuing Great Depression, when the devastation of personal fortunes induced a change of ownership in this section of valley. Around this time, lawyer and budding oilman Eric L. Harvie attained the land and found in it a sanctuary. Eric's son, Neil, took over in the 1950s, running

cattle on the original property, and added greatly to the ranch's size. Neil's children, Pauli Smith, Carol Raymond, Katie Harvie, and Tim Harvie, have carried out their father's wish to see the original part of the ranch preserved. In this way, the story of the park originates alongside the traditions of conservation, stewardship, and philanthropy that have long existed within the Harvie family.

Glenbow Ranch Provincial Park is 1,314 hectares (3,247 acres) of fescue grassland and foothills parkland on the north side of the Bow River Valley. It occupies fourteen kilometres of the Bow River shore between the city of Calgary and the town of Cochrane. For those unfamiliar

Silverberry, also known as wolf willow: a signature wild shrub in the valleys of southern Alberta.

with Canadian places, this is in the southern half of the province of Alberta, Canada.

From the river's curving north shore, the land rises gradually in long grassy terraces and benches until it reaches the foot of the valley's south-facing slope. From there north, the rise is steep: hills and cliffs clawed deeply by coulees. On the terraces, fescue and little bluestem are precious survivors of the short-grass prairie that once clothed the entire western Canadian prairie. In the shady sinuous coulees, buckbrush, silverberry, aspen, and many bird and animal species thrive. Cattle still graze here as they have done since 1881. On the map of the park, the northern border shows jogs and a long spike. These are coulee systems preserved from head to fan by the lines enclosing the park.

To appreciate the unlikeliness of this park, we need to consider the entire Bow River system and the previous century of its history. The headwaters and upper reaches of the Bow are preserved in Banff National Park, Canada's original federal park, but, below Banff National Park's east boundary, the river and its valley are heavily and complexly used. In the Bow Valley Basin above Glenbow Ranch Provincial Park are four hydroelectric dams, three major towns, and a First Nations reserve. Immediately below the park is the city of Calgary, and, beyond

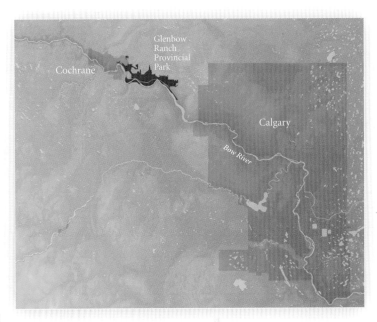

Calgary, another First Nations reserve and three irrigation districts. Approximately 1.25 million people live in the Bow River watershed, and 28 per cent of Alberta's agricultural output comes from land irrigated by the Bow.

That, at the beginning of the twenty-first century, a park of Glenbow Ranch's size could come into existence in such an intensely used space is beyond extra-ordinary. On the open market, this land would have been snapped up at premium prices in no time; cut into acreages, and filled with homes. Instead, the Harvie family's vision and generosity made it possible for the Government of Alberta to purchase the land for this park for about 60 per cent of its market assessment.

Glenbow Ranch Provincial park is 1,314 hectares of wild prairie on the north shore of the Bow River, just upstream of Calgary, Alberta: a modern city with over a million residents.

Glenbow Ranch Provincial Park

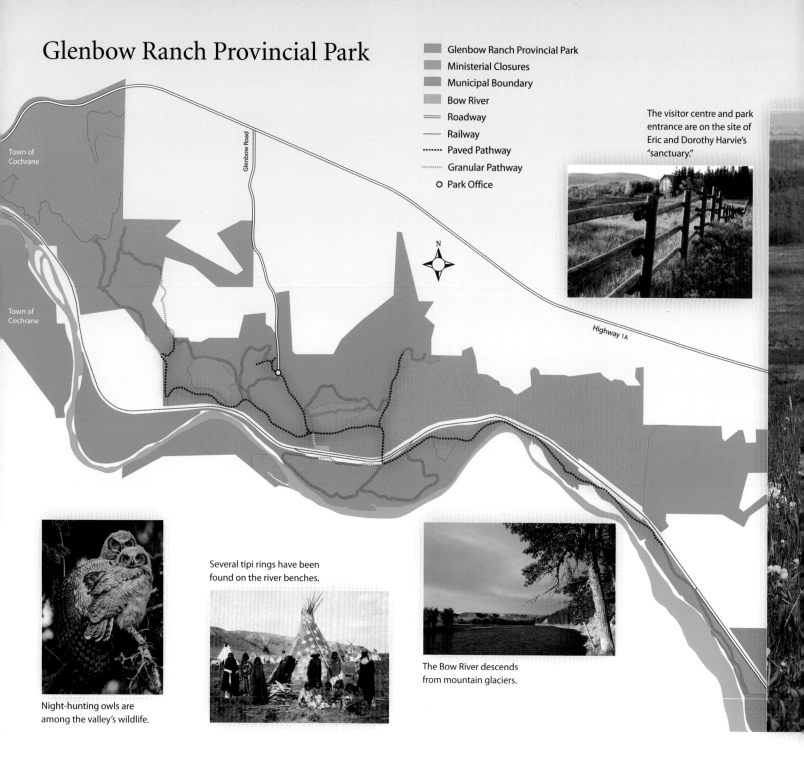

- ▬ Glenbow Ranch Provincial Park
- ▬ Ministerial Closures
- ▬ Municipal Boundary
- ▬ Bow River
- ═══ Roadway
- ⋯⋯ Railway
- ●●● Paved Pathway
- ⋯⋯ Granular Pathway
- ○ Park Office

Town of Cochrane

Town of Cochrane

Glenbow Road

N

Highway 1A

The visitor centre and park entrance are on the site of Eric and Dorothy Harvie's "sanctuary."

Night-hunting owls are among the valley's wildlife.

Several tipi rings have been found on the river benches.

The Bow River descends from mountain glaciers.

The remaining 40 per cent of the value was the family's gift.

The truth is that Glenbow Ranch Provincial Park defies every pattern of conventional growth, and yet it is exactly what southern Alberta society most needed: a place close to the hum of the city where Albertans can contemplate their past, present, and future; where people from other places can learn what southern Alberta is and has been in a deeper longer sense.

Though the park will appear to its visitors as a pastoral place, a grazing land where development is kept at bay, history tells a different story. If all Glenbow Ranch Provincial Park's human history could be witnessed at once, visitors would see early hunters and gatherers following the retreat of glacial ice; First Nations people of later times hunting bison in the coulees and camped in tipis on the terraces and high bluffs. They would see the cowboys and cattle of Canada's first open-range ranch lease; the construction of a section of the original Canadian Pacific Railway; the quarrying of sandstone for Alberta's Legislature Building; a colony of wealthy New York City millionaires playing polo with locals; a grain elevator, a brickyard, and a popular store in the ambitious village of Glenbow. These traces of 11,000 years of history add greatly to the value of the park.

The book in your hands is part of the celebration of Glenbow Ranch Provincial Park. The book's purpose is to introduce and display some of what is being preserved: not just a landscape but a storehouse of nature's genius; not just a natural history but a social history; not just ecology and history but an opportunity to see, participate, and learn, now and in the future.

Glenbow Ranch Provincial Park's greatest legacy may be as a model of stewardship that others can follow. If such a park can be founded in the Bow Valley, on the fringes of a surging city, then, truly, anything is possible.

Glenbow Ranch Provincial Park ... a place close to the hum of the city where Albertans can contemplate their past, present, and future.

Bow River

THE WORLD POPULARITY OF ALBERTA'S Royal Tyrrell Museum of Palaeontology has given an impression that dinosaur remains must litter the surface of southern Alberta; unearthed regularly by cultivators and garden shovels. But the dinosaur age has nothing to do with the history of Glenbow Ranch Provincial Park because the park's valley and river did not exist that long ago. Both were made in a more recent time: in the wake of the last glaciers, 18,000 years ago.

The last period of glaciation in North America featured two enormous ice sheets. The Laurentide Ice Sheet originated in the Labrador-Ungava plateau and centred over Hudson Bay. The farthest westward extent of the Laurentide Ice Sheet covered most of Alberta. The second ice sheet, the Cordilleran, filled and overflowed the Rocky Mountains. During their final advance, the two glaciers met, and, by then, most of future-Canada was covered and depressed by their frozen weight.

Prior to the final surge of the Cordilleran Ice Sheet, an ancient river exited the mountains not far from the present-day Bow River; but it did not follow the same path as the modern Bow. The ancient river left the mountains

through the valley that cradles Lake Minnewanka in Banff National Park. When the Cordilleran Ice Sheet finally retreated from the area, the glacial meltwater found a new way through the landscape: along the route of what became the Bow River.

When the ice was gone, the landscape would have been far from flat or uniform, for it contained everything the glacier had ploughed and collected. When the

Meltwater swept the valley full of rock and sediment. The young river carved through it. The benches you see here are the remnants of this repeating cycle.

The Big Rock at Okotoks, Alberta, is the world's largest known glacial erratic; part of a north-south trail of such rocks that marks where the Laurentide and the Cordilleran ice sheets met. The trail of erratics passes through Glenbow Ranch Provincial Park and one erratic has been found there.

Below are two types of rock found in the Bow Valley. The upper sample, a Quartz Arenite, is from a glacial erratic, borne south from the Jasper area. The lower sample is sandstone, a common bedrock in the Bow Valley.

Stones in the Bow Valley are often decorated by colourful crustose lichens.

erratic came to rest within the boundaries of Glenbow Ranch Provincial Park, after being carried three hundred kilometres by the Cordilleran ice from Mount Edith Cavell in Jasper National Park.

Into this landscape of glacial till the meltwaters of the last Cordilleran ice retreat were unleashed, ploughing, pooling, and braiding through the obstacle course, borne east and down by gravity.

If you were to stand on the high northern edge of the modern Bow Valley, a chasm of several kilometres yawns between you and the mirroring escarpment of the valley's southern edge. The modern Bow River, curving along the valley bottom, seems too small to be responsible for such a great span. The distant escarpment

Cordilleran Ice Sheet withdrew for the last time, it dropped boulders from its base, some the size of houses. Science was able to locate the frontier along which the two ice sheets met by studying the track of these mountain-born glacial erratics. One

was once the southern shoreline of glacial Lake Calgary (created by glacial meltwater). The huge valley is a testament to the Bow River's birth size rather than its present size; the barrelling power of its early millennia.

From the same hilltop vantage, you can see benches at different heights jutting from the valley walls. These are illustrations of stages in the valley's formation. To greatly oversimplify the process: the valley was ploughed by huge meltwater flows, filled with glacial tills, incised by the young river, filled again with sands and silts, carved again by water—and so on. The topmost benches are the oldest, and each bench is a memorial to a stable time within the valley's long life.

The soil that now coats the valley, in which the valley's flora grows, is another product of the Last Glacial Maximum.

The soil's ancestor is glacial dust known as *loess*, an ancient German word meaning "loose." The wind-borne dust coursed along the glaciers' surfaces, and, as the ice withdrew, drifted shallowly or deeply onto the exposed rock. The angular grains of crystal and mineral eventually united with wind-borne seeds from the unglaciated world. Over thousand-year sweeps of time, the vegetation became more complex, finally yielding the world we see.

Among the winners in this evolutionary struggle was a grass called fescue whose genius includes an amazing patience with moisture. When necessary, fescue can withdraw into its own roots and outwait the longest droughts. Aspen and willow seeds also landed in this valley niche and thrived.

The floral dressing of this landscape has been governed by climate and landform, with the Rocky Mountains as a primary influence. The eastward flow of moist Pacific air is forced high by the mountains and is milked of rain and snow across the Continental Divide. The air mass that continues eastward is still warm but much drier (a wind phenomenon of summer and winter known as the Chinook). At Glenbow Ranch Provincial Park, the resulting aridity is everywhere apparent, but especially so on the sun-baked walls of the cliffs and the south-facing grasslands. Another author of climate is the south-flowing Arctic air that makes winter at this latitude and altitude.

Above: Glacial silt and rock welded into conglomerate over time.

Right: As the Bow River valley carved downward and eroded along its walls, bands of sandstone were revealed.

Opposite page: A coyote sits on a hill carved into sections by thousands of years of erosion.

The glacial advances and retreats that brought the Bow River and Bow Valley into being are far in the past, but there is a sense in which the Ice Age still exists. Though climate change is diminishing the remnants of the glaciers in the mountains, it is still possible for a visitor to Glenbow Ranch Provincial Park to visit the Bow River's birthplace. In Banff National Park, on the Icefields Highway north of Lake Louise, Bow Lake stands below Bow Glacier. Water that runs from the toe of this glacier will eventually pass through Glenbow Ranch.

For the record, if you also wanted to visit the remains of the Laurentide Ice Sheet, a much longer journey would be required. The final remnant of the Laurentide is Barnes Ice Cap, found on Baffin Island: Canada's oldest ice.

After the melting of the glaciers, it was not long before animals re-entered the landscape in pursuit of green. Between the retreating ice sheets (approximately 13,000 years ago), the vegetated landscape would have been tundra-like, and dotted with meltwater lakes. It is believed that incoming animals arrived from the south: species that had been kept out of north-ern North America by ice for several millennia.

Extraordinary archaeological finds have been made in southern Alberta where the seam of the ice sheets parted. At a location called Wally's Beach, at St. Mary's Reservoir, an ancient biological tableau came to light during a temporary draining of the water body. Silt and sand blew off to reveal remnants of ancient camels, Mexican horses, mammoths, mastodons, and a sabre-tooth cat. Also revealed were complex trackways: evidence left by living creatures. By these tracks, researchers have been able to define the size and age of the community of ancient elephants that passed this way. Even the frolic between young elephants was recorded in compressed sand. The speed of the ancient elephants' gait could be deduced. The number of young in the group was

Bones of ancient camels, horses, and woolly mammoths have been found in Bighill Creek Formation gravels not far from Glenbow Ranch Provincial Park.

abnormally low, a sign of an animal community under stress. This tallies with the fact that most large animals of the late Pleistocene were nearing extinction in North America at the time. Their north-ward trek might have been a desperate attempt to survive.

Wally's Beach is about a 2.5 hour drive south of Glenbow Ranch Provincial Park. Though the mix of animals is somewhat different, an excavation far closer to Glenbow Ranch (Cochrane Gravel Pit; Churcher, 1968, 1975) unearthed animals from the same Pleistocene-Holocene timeframe. In the gravel pit were traces of a camel, an ancient bison, a Mexican horse, and a large mountain sheep. The fossils are believed to be 13,000 years old.

A great mystery to the scientists who study the ancient past is why so many of the earliest large animals of North America died out. The horse, which had evolved in North America, was one of those species that disappeared from the North American continent thousands of years ago. Camel, mastodon, mammoth, and a species of giant beaver the size of a modern bear, also vanished.

Luckily, before its extinction in North America, enough horses escaped across the land bridge to Asia to perpetuate the species. (During the Ice Age, this land bridge connected North America and Asia.) The horse returned to North America in the fifteenth century CE on Spanish ships.

A host of other animal species used the Ice Age land bridge to cross in the other direction: from Asia into North America. Bears and many kinds of ungulates came. Many of the wild species within Glenbow Ranch Provincial Park are products of that migration.

Part of the excitement of Glenbow Ranch Provincial Park is the geological history expressed in its landforms and exposed walls of rock. As time passes, generations of scientists will examine the park, and the story of its history will grow.

Right: Through the work of archaeologists, geologists, biologists–all manner of scientists and historians–our knowledge of Glenbow Ranch Provincial Park is destined to grow.

First Nations on the Bow

THE QUESTION OF WHEN THE FIRST HUMAN beings may have walked along the valley of the Bow River cannot be answered. Or, rather, it has been answered, compellingly, but in two opposing ways. Both versions suggest that the first humans crossed the land bridge from Asia (a thousand-kilometre wide strip of land exposed by the Ice Age drop in the level of oceans), and that these people came in pursuit of large mammals like ancient elephants, which were also entering North America across the land bridge.

From here the stories diverge. Let's call the first version *Ice-free Corridor*. In this story, the migrants from Asia continued south into North America through an ice-free corridor along the east slope of the Rocky Mountains: an unglaciated space between the ice sheets. In this way, they reached the ice-free southern portion of North America, where they spread across the continent and continued into South America. All this was believed to have occurred about 13,000 years ago.

Then came scientific evidence that this was impossible—at least impossible at this particular time. Researchers had discovered that the earliest human occupation of southern North America coincided with the six thousand years during which the Laurentide and Cordilleran Ice Sheets were tight together for a thousand kilometres: a barrier that could not have been traversed.

This *No Ice-free Corridor* version suggests that the first North Americans came in the same time interval (13,000 years ago) but by some other route, perhaps along the coastlines, which were also expanded by the low level of the oceans.

In 2011, reports of a new find in Texas suggested something entirely different. An excavation called the Buttermilk Complex has yielded almost 16,000 human-related artefacts that scientific methods suggest are 15,500 years old—two thousand years older than most other early human sites and artefacts. If this is the beginning of a new first-people story for North America, the *Ice-free Corridor* version could be back in contention, with a different timeline.

In Alberta, the earliest finds of human artefacts, made thus far, have been in the 11,000- to 12,000-year-old range. These

Left: Blackfoot encampment, southern Alberta, c. 1890.

The coyote: a trickster figure in many First Nations legends.

Minnewanka did produce fragments of Clovis points.

The dating of these sites suggests that Clovis people did not come into Alberta from the north but from the south. That is, the evidence suggests they were in southern North America already and followed prey animals north into the newly vegetated territory between the parting ice sheets. Into this rocky, flooded, tundra-like terrain, the Stone Age hunters came on foot, walking the shores of glacial lakes. At Vermilion Lakes, an ancient hearth was found, surrounded by burned and broken bones of large mountain sheep and elk or caribou. The Clovis people camped here may have used the steaming hot springs that still pool at the foot of nearby Sulphur Mountain.

Along the Bow River and nearby are other Clovis sites. At Sibbald Flats—a grassy terrace an hour's drive west-southwest of Glenbow Ranch Provincial Park—an 11,000-year-old, green, siltstone, spear point was found. While it had the Clovis flutes chipped out of its sides, the point was also different from classic Clovis points in that it was shorter. "Stubbies" has become the name for this variation on the point, and it continues to be found in western Canadian excavations dated to this time.

The discovery of 15,000-year-old human artefacts in Texas means that we cannot definitely say that the Clovis people were the first people in southern

finds relate to a people of Asian origin that we call Clovis. We identify artefacts as being from the Clovis culture if they are accompanied by the fluted and flaked stone spear points this people used to kill large mammals (such as the Asian mammoth and the North American mastodon). A rich Clovis site found at Vermilion Lakes in the upper Bow River contained many layers of human occupation. The deepest and oldest layer is thought to be 11,800 years old. Though no Clovis spear points were found at Vermilion Lakes, a dig at nearby Lake

Basally-thinned "stubby" spear points (top and middle) and a Midland spear point (bottom) from lower levels of the Sibbald Creek Site located in the southern foothills about seventy kilometres west of Calgary.

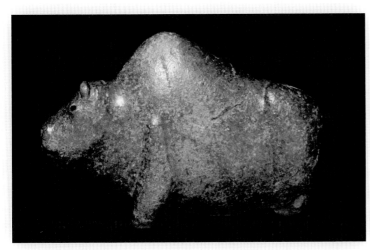

This extremely rare green quartzite buffalo effigy was found in central Alberta in 1960. It is believed that the First Nation artist carved it between 500 and 1,000 years ago.

Alberta; rather, they were the earliest people we know about. If human artefacts are found relating to an earlier time, when there was an ice-free corridor through Alberta, the whole story will change again.

An irony of the arrival of the Clovis people in the Bow Valley and vicinity is that many of the great mammals they were pursuing were on their way to extinction. The Wally's Beach site in southern Alberta revealed stone tools used to kill and butcher horses, solid evidence that human hunters had been killing and eating horses and may have contributed to the horse's extirpation in North America. Whether humans were the main cause of such large-mammal extirpations and extinctions will go on being debated, but it is true that North American mastodons, mammoths, camels, Mexican horses, giant bison, sloths, and giant beavers all disappeared from North America in the early Holocene period, when humans were present.

After the glaciers began their long retreat, the climate and vegetation of western Canada changed. The glacial lakes shrank to their modern size or simply disappeared. Spruce forests replaced tundra. When the climate became warmer and drier still, the evergreen forests withdrew into the shadows as grasslands spread in the sun.

The changes in the land meant that humans had to change, as well. The early people of the forests tended to rely on many animals, including fish. Those who inhabited the grasslands lived almost exclusively off one animal: the bison. To some degree all early people learned to gather edible plants, as insurance against failures in the hunt and to add useful vitamins and medicines to their diets.

Rivers like the Bow were essential to First Nations life.

For the ten thousand-plus years we know people have lived in this region, the Bow Valley would have always been a preferred place: a source of food, fuel, and water. Through what is now Glen-bow Ranch Provincial Park, continuous migrations of animals and humans must have passed, going upstream and down. On the low terraces and hilltops, the ancient travellers camped, leaving their fire-broken rocks, and the bones of the prey animals they hunted.

The First Nations people who live in the Bow River drainage today all descend from this saga, though not necessarily in the same ways. The Blackfoot (Siksika, Kainai, and Pikuni) moved west until

Archaeology

When you look from the cliffs and hilltops of Glenbow Ranch Provincial Park into the valley, at the river and the aspen-clad interior hills, no scar in the landscape, no structure, cries out from the First Nations' past. The early people were not builders in the European sense, and the physical signs of their presence are easily hidden by the soil and the grass. It is largely left to our imaginations to repopulate the coulees and terraces with grazing bison, painted tipis, fires, and human society.

Archaeology has its own ways of contacting and reproducing the past. Two archaeological surveys of the Bow Valley at this location have identified prehistoric sites within or close to the boundaries of Glenbow Ranch Provincial Park. Prehistoric, in this sense, means 150 years ago: the time before the Europeans joined the First Nations on this landscape; the time before written history.

The last archaeological survey of the Glenbow Ranch Provincial Park area, in 2007, found twenty-seven prehistoric First Nations sites. Most are called "stone features," meaning uses of stone by First Nations people. The features contain tipi rings and mark places where people camped. They used the stones to weight the lower edges of their hide tipis against the wind. The number of tipi

circles (in excess of twenty-five) suggests the size of the community. On average, up to eight people lived in each tent.

Artefacts at these sites tend to be related to the flintknapper's art: the making of tools and weapons by flaking one rock with another. These artefacts may be flakes struck from lithic *cores*: rocks from which flakes have been struck.

Another artefact type is fire-broken rock. Stones were used not only to crib campfires but also in pits to boil meat and in sweat lodges to produce steam and heat.

Looked at on a map, the prehistoric campsites in the park tend to relate to two physical features: river terraces and hilltops. These were the preferred places to camp: close to water and firewood, or up high where one could see far.

Neither the survey of 1973 nor the more recent 2007 one involved excavation. Because of the care taken by the previous owners of this land and because the area is best suited for grazing, the sites tend not to have been disturbed. For that reason they have been given a high archaeological value. The change from private property to provincial park means that no unwanted disturbance will happen in the future either. It is exciting to think what careful scientific approaches might discover within this section of the Bow Valley in the future.

they dominated the western prairie and mountain approaches. They are believed to be descended from those who organized the huge seasonal hunts at bison jumps like Head-Smashed-In and Old Women's.

The Mountain Assiniboine who live in the Bow Valley fifty kilometres west of Glenbow Ranch Provincial Park are descended from eastern woodland tribes. Probably in the eighteenth century, the Mountain Assiniboine split off from the Plains Assiniboine and came to the east slope of the Rocky Mountains. The Assiniboine are related to the American Sioux and speak a similar Siouan language.

On the river benches of Glenbow Ranch Provincial Park, many tipi rings have been found, circles of rocks roughly uniform in size that the Plains First Nations used to hold their tipi covers to the ground in the face of heavy winds.

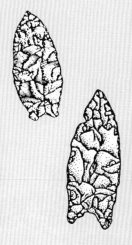

Timelines

To look at the ten-thousand-year span of human activity in the Bow Valley has
an interesting impact on one's perspective. The image most of us have of the First
Nations is the warrior, with spear and feather headdress, astride a galloping horse
or posed on a cliff top. These are grand images, but we need to remember that the
"horse days" represent less than half of 1 per cent of the total time the First Nations
have lived here. Even their "dog days" (when domesticated dogs helped carry
their goods from camp to camp) did not come until three thousand years of life in
North America had passed. What we know about the millennia of First Nations life
on this continent is very little. Even the length of time people have lived here
remains a subject of debate.

The Tsuu T'ina First Nation, who live southwest of Calgary, were bison hunters and nineteenth-century allies of the Blackfoot Confederacy, but they were originally Beaver people in Canada's north. They speak an Athapaskan language.

The Kootenai First Nation of the interior of British Columbia once lived here, too. Their bark-sided tipis were observed in the mountain foothills by early European explorers.

Modern archaeology continues to define the ancestors of these first First Nations by diagnostic artefacts, such as weapon points. Possessions like pottery, bison stones, and pipestones also help to map their movement through time, as well as to show the wide range of trading that went on. Obsidian toolstone used by the peoples of the Canadian plains came from the Dakotas and Wyoming. Shells worn for decoration came from as far away as the Gulf of Mexico.

The first great change in North American weapon technology began around 8,500 years ago. The spear points up to this time had equipped thrusting spears, but the new wave of points had side notches and stems for tying to a wooden shaft.

> Shells worn for decoration came from as far away as the Gulf of Mexico.

These were throwing spears and employed a throwing board, or atlatl.

The artefacts found with these points begin to unfold the history of First Nations culture. Painted bison skulls and medicine bundles decorated with red ochre speak of a complex spiritual life.

In their book *First Peoples in Canada*, authors Alan D. McMillan and Eldon Yellowhorn (a Pikuni First Nation archaeologist) write of how the First Nations themselves define their history. The Blackfoot divide their past into the "dog days" and the "horse days," based on which animal they depended on to move their goods.

Some of the richest artefact finds have been made at the foot of long-used bison jumps. The classic jump in southern Alberta is Head-Smashed-In, now a UNESCO World Heritage Site. Two hour's drive south of Glenbow Ranch Provincial Park, and just north of the Oldman River, Head-Smashed-In was used by the First Nations across a six-thousand-year span. The system of the seasonal hunts that culminated in a spill of animals over the sandstone cliffs was subtle, systematic, and demanded great knowledge of the bison and of the local landforms. The hunt began far back in the labyrinthine Porcupine Hills where young people covered themselves in hides and impersonated bawling bison calves. They lured the grazing bison into drive lanes marked by stone cairns, always careful not to panic the herd. Only when the bison were close to the cliffs did people hiding behind the cairns rise up, shout, and flap robes. The stampeding bison ran off the cliff. At the bottom, the people waited with spears and sharpened butchering tools to finish the bison off and begin the meat harvest.

Another asset of Head-Smashed-In was that it had a spring at the base of the cliffs, a water source that allowed people to live easily while the meat and hides were processed. Some of the bison meat was boiled in pits and eaten by those gathered for the hunt. Most of the meat would have been hung on frames over smoky fires to make dry meat that could last and travel.

The First Nations made remarkably thorough use of the bison; every part from hair to brains to stomach to sinews to bones to horns was employed in their material, decorative, and spiritual culture.

In the last two thousand years of the dog days, people known to archaeology as Besant learned that the rise of the Lost Boys constellation (Pleiades) meant it was bison-calving season. The appearance of the Lost Boys on the horizon was the signal to leave the wintering camps and start for Head-Smashed-In and the other jumps, so the painstaking process of luring and guiding the bison on foot could begin again.

Another surviving feature of ancient life on the plains is the medicine wheel. On high prairie hills, medicine wheels of various sizes and designs have been found. Most have a central cairn and rock lines radiating out. Others form pictures of animals and people. The Plains Indians of western Canada also drew pictographs and carved petroglyphs. The best surviving examples of these are drawn on and into the sandstone walls and hoodoos at Writing-On-Stone in south central Alberta, across the 49th parallel from the American Sweetgrass Hills.

Three thousand years into the human history of this locale, a second great shift of weapon technology took place: from throwing spear to bow and arrow.

The ability of hunters to hit moving targets was greatly improved. But an even greater change came when the Spanish returned the horse to its ancestral home in the fifteenth and sixteenth centuries CE. The reintroduction of the horse revolutionized First Nations life.

The first horses to wander into the orbit of Canada's First Nations arrived around 1730. Domestication was swift. Though initially called an Elk Dog or Big Dog, because it could carry burdens, the horse was soon re-adapted for riding. As an equestrian people, the Blackfoot enjoyed their greatest success. Bison could be hunted on horseback, with bow and arrow, and without the complex organization of a bison jump. The Plains tribes enjoyed a surplus of meat and robes, even horses, which they could trade with other Natives and eventually with white fur traders.

The horse literally accelerated First Nations history, changing standards of bravery, wealth, and glory; increasing the frequency and lethality of war. This was also the advent of the first meeting with white Europeans—but that in every way is another story.

Amidst bison bones, rare and intricate pottery fragments have been found that give insight into Native lifestyles.

Two Worlds Meet

EARLY CONTACT BETWEEN ALBERTA'S FIRST Nations and Europeans changed the First Nations world. But one of the ironies of such a momentous change was how few marks the social, cultural, and economic shifts made on the land itself: deeper ruts from wheeled carts and wagons; a few fort palisades left rotting in the ground.

Temporarily, contact with Europeans seemed beneficial for the First Nations, because the Europeans were traders willing to part with never-before-seen goods in exchange for beaver skins (an animal that was not even a valuable food animal). The gun and horse created a new circumstance for plains Aboriginal peoples: material surplus. With horses they could move faster and kill more bison; carry more possessions from camp to camp. But then came liquor, disease, and the depletion of the bison: plagues with the power to wipe out health, food, and life.

Because of the transience of both traders and plains First Nations, it is not possible to say when the first European and the first Native met in the part of the Bow River valley that is now Glenbow Ranch Provincial Park. One of the earliest meetings along the Bow involved a group of Pikuni and Hudson's Bay Company employee David Thompson in the winter of 1787–88. Thompson was just seventeen and had been sent by the HBC to winter with the Pikuni people. Thompson was an orphaned English lad who had been educated in a charity school in London. As an HBC apprentice, his winter with the Pikuni was his opportunity to learn an important Indian tribe's language and culture, and to forge alliances among them.

David Thompson would go on to become a renowned fur-trade surveyor and map-maker. As well, he was a chronicler of his times, whose diaries and memoirs have been greatly relied upon by historians. From those writings, we know that Thompson befriended an elder named Saukamapee that winter and that Saukamapee told him stories ranging back to the early eighteenth century. Saukamapee was a Cree who had spent much of his life with the Blackfoot-speaking Pikuni. He told of a battle between the Blackfoot and the Snake Indians (Shoshone) around 1720, in which the Blackfoot had received the majority of wounds because their war shields were so much

The Plains First Nations had always been trading people, but the goods brought by European fur traders were made of iron: forks, knives, needles, metal spear and arrow points, bullets, and guns. Their world was changed through trade.

Story robes, or winter counts, like this one kept by Raw Eater, tell the story of First Nations history from their own perspective. Some are extremely old and bear witness to events like inter-tribal battles and smallpox plagues.

smaller than those of their enemies. Both sides were fighting with bow and arrow, and no one was killed.

Around this time, the Cree acquired muzzle-loading guns from the HBC. When visiting the Blackfoot, the Cree offered to lend the assistance of their new weapon if there was another war against the Shoshone. That battle occurred around 1730, and, when the Cree fired their guns, the Shoshone fled. Saukamapee's story, written down by David Thompson, is the first account in English of the use of the gun in the war history of a Blackfoot Nation.

In the year following David Thompson's winter with the Pikuni, the fur trader so badly broke a leg that he almost lost the limb and his life. Later, when studying to be a surveyor, he looked at the sun too long and lost the sight in one eye. But these afflictions did not cost him his ambition. Near the end of the eighteenth century, he was frustrated enough by the relative inaction of the HBC to cross over to their only competitor, the North West Company. As a Nor'wester, Thompson returned to the Bow River in 1800. This expedition intersected the Bow at or near its confluence with the Elbow River (the modern site of Calgary). From here, the traders turned west and followed the river to the mountains. So it is that David Thompson must have passed through or near what is now Glenbow Ranch Provincial Park.

Between Thompson's two visits to the Bow, another HBC-trained surveyor, Peter Fidler, also made a foray into this area.

No historical image of map-maker David Thompson has ever been found, so artist C.W. Jefferys created this one. David Thompson was likely one of the first Europeans to walk west up the valley of the Bow in the eighteenth century.

In 1792–93, Fidler crossed the Bow in the company of Pikuni guides and continued south to the place where the Oldman River exits the Rocky Mountains. The steep-sided zigzag cut through the mountain is known today as the Gap, and Fidler and his HBC colleague John Ward were the first Europeans to record a passage through it. On the Gap's west side the explorers met members of the Kootenai First Nation, who had never seen a Caucasian before. Fidler wrote in his diary that he and Ward were thoroughly inspected.

On Peter Fidler's return journey, his Pikuni guides led him north between the Livingstone Range and the Porcupine Hills, and eventually back to and across the Bow River.

Though Thompson's and Fidler's forays are written proof that the fur trade was somewhat active in the Bow River drainage by the late eighteenth century, no fur-trading fort was built in Blackfoot country during the four decades following Thompson's first visit. The main reason was fear of the Blackfoot-speaking tribes who dominated the region. The land bounded by the Red Deer River, the Missouri River, and the Rocky Mountains was excellent bison-hunting country, and the Blackfoot controlled it by maintaining a state of hot or cold war with all the tribes beyond. Though Saukamapee's story suggests a time when the Blackfoot and Cree were friendly, they were far from it for most of the nineteenth century. The last battle between the two occurred in 1870 on the steep banks of the Oldman River (above which the city of Lethbridge now stands), with the Pikuni and Kainai winning a decisive victory.

Rather than build forts and trade within the Blackfoot Confederacy domain, the North West Company and the Hudson's Bay Company preferred to lure the Blackfoot to forts along the North Saskatchewan River. There the two competing companies built their forts side by side, so the other company would not have an advantage at the location. This situation lasted until 1821 when the two warring companies merged under the Hudson's Bay Company name.

After amalgamation, the HBC forts closest to Blackfoot country were Fort Edmonton and Rocky Mountain House,

Fort Edmonton was the Saskatchewan District headquarters of the Hudson's Bay Company. The First Nations along the Bow River were expected to go there, or to Rocky Mountain House, to trade. Instead, they eventually went to the Americans on the Missouri River and HBC trade on the prairies declined.

A fur trader and his Métis guide travelling by snowshoe.

Left: Artist William Armstrong accompanied Sir Sanford Fleming to the Rocky Mountains in 1877. In this painting, he depicts a Blackfoot encampment at the foot of the mountains.

A Paul Kane painting of Fort Edmonton, as it appeared in 1846. A crew was dispatched from Fort Edmonton to establish Peigan Post on the Bow River in 1833.

both on the North Saskatchewan River. The Pikuni, Kainai, and Siksika continued to bring their skins and bison meat to these forts because they had no choice. Since the Lewis and Clark expedition had killed a Blackfoot in 1806, the Blackfoot Confederacy had maintained a state of war with the Americans and rebuffed every attempt by Americans to build fur forts along the Missouri. Hence, it was either trade north with the HBC or not trade at all.

What led to the first Hudson's Bay Company fort on the Bow River was a softening of the Blackfoot position toward the Americans. In the late 1820s, the American Fur Company built new forts on the upper Missouri, and the Blackfoot let them stand. One reason the Blackfoot made this peace was so that they would no longer have to cross enemy territory to get to the HBC forts. Another factor was that the HBC had greatly lowered its prices after the 1821 amalgamation. The Americans were much more generous in their attempt to secure the Blackfoot trade.

When the Blackfoot stopped going north it was a significant loss to the HBC. Though the Blackfoot were not a major source of beaver skins (to be made into beaver hats in Britain and Europe: the HBC's major trade good), they were the best supplier of the high-protein food called pemmican. Pemmican was a mixture of dried bison meat (ground to powder), wild berries, and bison fat, and it literally fuelled the paddlers of the boats that carried the trade goods upriver to the forts and the skins downriver to the

> … in 1833, the HBC did what it had never done before; it entered deep into Blackfoot country and built a fur fort.

Atlantic. The HBC could not continue to operate if they could not rely on the Blackfoot trade in pemmican.

Therefore, in 1833, the HBC did what it had never done before; it entered deep into Blackfoot country and built a fur fort. Peigan Post was built on the Bow River near the mountains (west of Glenbow Ranch Provincial Park, in what is now the Stoney First Nation). The man in charge of the post was Edward Harriott, a veteran fur trader who had come from England decades before at the age of twelve. But Harriott could not handle the hot potato the company had thrown him. The HBC had made the awkward decision that Peigan Post would be solely for the Pikuni (Peigan), while the other members of the Blackfoot Confederacy—the Siksika, Kainai, and Tsuu T'ina—would continue trading at the North Saskatchewan forts. Peigan Post was closer and safer for all these tribes, and the Siksika and Kainai determined that if they could not trade there, neither would the Pikuni. The situation became steadily more threatening until Harriott gave up and returned to Rocky Mountain House.

The following season, Harriott was sent to try again. But the same Pikuni-only rule doomed the venture. This time an actual battle between the Kainai and the Pikuni caused the closing of the fort in mid-winter. It would never open again, and no other HBC post was attempted in Blackfoot country until the coming of

Canada's mounted police (known today as the Royal Canadian Mounted Police).

The next European entrants on the Bow River stage were Christian missionaries. The Methodist missionary Robert Rundle came to Fort Edmonton and Rocky Mountain House in 1840 and, after considerable success among the Mountain Assiniboine and Strongwood Cree, he arranged an expedition into Blackfoot country in 1842. He met the Kainai on the banks of the Bow River. Again there is no specific land location data that would define where this meeting took place, but just prior to intersecting the Bow, Rundle was taken to a place called Writing Rocks, which might have referred to the tufa stone at Big Hill Springs, north of Glenbow Ranch.

The history of western Canada, and the Bow Valley along with it, took a sudden veer toward the present when the Hudson's Bay Company gave up its huge trading monopoly to the young nation of Canada in 1869. To be part of a nation rather than a fur-trading wilderness meant eventual, inevitable development, but in the early years under Canadian rule, the part of the West that is now southern Alberta was convulsed by the very opposite of development: a destructive whisky trade.

By 1869, trading alcohol to First Nations people was prohibited on both sides of the border. The US Government

Robert Rundle and the Blackfoot

When Methodist missionary Robert Rundle met his first Blackfoot-speaking congregation on the Bow River (likely not far from Glenbow Ranch Provincial Park) things did not go well. Rundle's interpreter into Blackfoot, a Métis named Jimmy Jock Bird, took offence and refused to interpret. Left to his own devices, Rundle could do nothing but sing. A dusty Chinook wind coming in under the sides of the tipi took away his voice, and the people silently left.

Though he was always welcome in the Blackfoot camps as long as he remained in the West, Reverend Rundle was never able to convert a Blackfoot-speaker. He continued to be successful in converting the Cree and Assiniboine, setting the stage for the Methodist missionaries who followed him.

Methodist missionary Robert Rundle came to the Bow River in 1842 to meet the Kanai people. In 1848, he returned to England where he settled and married. He wrote that he had never been able to baptize any of the Blackfoot-speaking people.

had passed legislation against it; the HBC had discontinued the practice. But when Canada took over from the HBC, and did nothing to assert its authority in the western part of its new domain, commercial interests in Montana saw an opportunity. Wagons full of spirits were hauled north across the Canada–US border into Blackfoot country.

From 1869 until well into 1873, this chaotic violent trade continued with no effective response from the Canadian government. At a large strong fort called Whoop-Up, and at a string of smaller whisky forts, all supplied by powerful merchants in Fort Benton, Montana, the First Nations traded bison hides for near-poisonous mixtures that went by the name of whisky. The Indians traded themselves into a profound state of poverty, made worse by a wave of small-pox that scorched the prairie in 1870.

The first flurry of whisky trading occurred along the Oldman River and its

tributaries, but the illicit trade began to work its way north. In 1872, whisky traders arrived at the confluence of the Elbow and the Bow Rivers (the future site of Calgary) and built a fort. In his book *Firewater*, Alberta historian Hugh Dempsey details what happened that winter. The first group of whisky traders, led by Americans Sol Abbott, Jim Scott, and Fred Kanouse, were trading with the Kainai when an argument started in the trade room. Both sides fired their guns. A trader named Muffraw was fatally shot and so was a Kainai. Fred Kanouse was hit badly in the shoulder. The Kainai escaped the fort and laid siege to it for three days.

A second fort opened not far away, operated by Donald Watson Davis, an American working for John Healy, one of the originators of Fort Whoop-Up. Davis's trade with the Kainai was somewhat less violent, perhaps because his wife, Revenge Walker, was a sister of the Kainai chief, Red Crow. Despite (or perhaps because of) his notoriously violent drinking episodes, Red Crow was one of the First Nations leaders who welcomed and assisted the mounted police when they arrived to suppress the whisky trade in 1874.

The beginning of the end for the whisky trade was a massacre of Assiniboine by white wolfers and traders in the Cypress Hills in 1873. It made the newspapers in eastern Canada and

Left: Crowfoot, a contemporary of Red Crow, was a Kanai born on the Belly River, but he became a main chief of the Siksika people. He was among the Blackfoot confederacy chiefs who welcomed the mounted police in 1874, to bring about an end to the deadly whisky trade.

Right: This staged and romanticized view of the mounted police force–First Nations relationship is based on the fact that the coming of the Mounties to western Canada in 1874 released the First Nations from the impoverishing grip of the whisky trade.

Fort Calgary, as painted by mounted police surgeon R.B. Nevitt in 1876. The Mounties at Fort Calgary scattered the whisky traders and made the area safe for ranching.

pressured John A. MacDonald, Canada's first prime minister, to act. He created Canada's mounted police force and sent them west. After a largely disastrous 1300-kilometre march from Manitoba to future-southern Alberta, the Mounties still had enough staying power to limit the whisky traders, most of whom made sudden conversions to honest business. The first mounted police fort in whisky country was Fort Macleod on the Oldman River (named for Colonel Macleod, who commanded the local force). Recognizing that the Bow River was also whisky-trading country, the Mounties built Fort Calgary at the Bow and Elbow in 1875.

The Death of George McDougall

George McDougall created several missions in western Canada for the Methodist Church. In 1872, his thirty-year-old son, John, followed George into the ministry, and the Morley mission on the Bow River was John's first project. Another son, David, a trader, went with John to Morley and set up a trading shop.

Methodist Mission at Morleyville, 1881.

The combination of a mission and a trading shop was a subject of derision among the whisky traders. They started a rumour, reported in the *Benton Record*, that David McDougall was trading while his brother preached. This was a lie.

When the Hudson's Bay Company saw the McDougalls living and trading safely on the Bow, they returned to the Bow River and set up a trading post at Ghost River. It was the HBC's first venture on the Bow since the Peigan Post disaster of 1834.

In 1876, tragedy came to the McDougall family. Reverend John, a vigorous frontiersman, organized a bison hunt in cold January weather. When one of John's party did not show up, his father George volunteered to replace the man. They had several sleds pulled by horses, and the prairie was glazed over with ice, making it difficult for a horse to run. Two of John's horses would not run the bison for fear of falling, and a third, which did run hard on the ice, had a dangerous fall. Still, John was able to kill several bison cows. They loaded the sleds and started back for camp. George said he would ride ahead to alert the camp and get things ready for the arrival of the sleds. It was the last time John McDougall saw his father alive. After a search that swept back and forth for several days, George McDougall's frozen remains were found on the upland northwest of Fort Calgary. It is hard to know exactly where George McDougall died, but, from the description John left in his memoir, *Opening the Great West*, his father's tragic death could not have been far from the north boundary of Glenbow Ranch Provincial Park.

First Nation seeding grain by hand in the 1880s. Thousands of years of civilization based on the buffalo had to change immediately if the prairie First Nations were to survive.

One of the whisky traders who became an honest businessman was Donald Watson Davis. He bossed the work crew that built Fort Calgary and went on to become a Canadian Member of Parliament.

But the Mounties were not the first non-Native opponents of the whisky trade to arrive along the Bow River. When the whisky trade was still flourishing in its power vacuum in 1873, the McDougall family came south from the Fort Edmonton area to establish a Methodist mission on the Bow River. At a popular ford above the confluence with the Ghost River, they built their mission for the Mountain Assiniboine (Stoneys) at Morleyville. The same year, Roman Catholic Father Constantine Scollen established Our Lady of Peace on the Elbow River (twenty kilometres south of Glenbow Ranch Provincial Park). Both the Methodist McDougalls and Father Scollen were loud voices of protest against the whisky trade.

When it purchased Rupert's Land from the Hudson's Bay Company, Canada's vision for the future was to somehow settle the huge prairie from Manitoba to the Rockies. The creation of the first mounted police force, ancestor to the Royal Canadian Mounted Police, was a prelude to that settlement: the first effort toward it. The next step was an agreement with the First Nations people by which they would relinquish their claim to most of the land the settlers would live on. This was the treaty process that worked its way from east to west through the 1870s. The last and biggest treaty was Number Seven. The negotiation and signing of the treaty took place in 1877 at Crowfoot Crossing on the Bow River, east of Calgary. There, the Siksika, Kainai, Pikuni, Tsuu T'ina, and Stoneys (Chiniki, Bearspaw, and Wesley/Goodstoney) met Canada's and the British Queen's representatives to discuss their future. After days of talking, the great chiefs marked their X and allowed what became the future to begin.

The Cochrane Ranche

On the far left of this 1903 round-up portrait, sitting a pale horse, is Dr. Duncan McNab McEachran: at one time the manager of both the Cochrane and the Waldron Ranches.

IN THE LATE NINETEENTH CENTURY, GLENBOW Ranch Provincial Park was part of the Cochrane Ranche: western Canada's first government lease ranch. Senator Matthew Cochrane of Compton, Quebec, owned the lease, and it was his December 1880 letter to Canada's Minister of the Interior that sparked Canada's lease-ranching frontier into existence. In his letter, Cochrane stated an intention to found a cattle ranch in the West. Three months later, a second letter modified his plan to include a one-hundred-thousand-acre (40,468-hectare) lease. What had inspired Senator Cochrane was a visit from Canadian Mounted Police Captain William Winder. Winder was also from Quebec but had spent much of his career as a mounted policeman at Fort Macleod. His message to Cochrane was that the wiping out of the buffalo had left a staggering amount of prairie grass without a big grazer—a rancher's dream.

Before the end of 1881, an Order in Council laying out the rules for western Canada's lease ranches became law. The terms were a penny per acre per year up to one hundred thousand acres. There was a stocking provision to ensure lessees intended to ranch. By the time the order was enacted, the Cochrane Ranche Company already existed, and Senator Cochrane was awarded the first lease.

The original Cochrane Ranche was in the Bow Valley upriver from Fort Calgary. Its big house, barns, and corrals were on the north side of the Bow River, at the foot of the "Big Hill." Big Hill Creek flowed through the home ranch, dividing the big house from the cowboys' bunkhouse and other buildings. All this is easily located today. In the town of Cochrane, a few kilometres west of Glenbow Ranch Provincial Park, the town's main park commemorates the ranch on its original site. The outline of the Cochrane big house is marked in wood at the foot of a small rocky hill. On top of that hill is a statue of a cowboy seated on his horse. The statue is named "Men of Vision."

Far right: Two and a half million bison were destroyed each year between 1870 and 1875. Homesteaders gathered the bones and hauled them to rail cars for much-needed extra income. Calcium from the bones was used for chalk and fertilizer.

Senator Matthew Cochrane

Left: Glenbow Ranch Provincial Park with the town of Cochrane in the background. Cochrane is named for the Cochrane Ranche, an 1880s lease ranch that once enveloped all of the present-day park.

Matthew Cochrane was no ingénue in the cattle business. Though his fortune was made in the leather industry, he was a prominent breeder of Shorthorn cattle in Quebec. In 1867, he imported from Britain two of the most celebrated Shorthorns the North American continent had ever seen. The following year, he imported another eleven Shorthorn Bates cattle. One Bates cow, Duchess 97, cost him a thousand guineas, a world-record price for a single cow at the time.

Though the Cochrane Ranche was the first lease ranch, it was not Alberta's first cattle ranch. The first cattle to come to the Bow River area were probably the ones that missionary John McDougall and his brother trailed south to their new Methodist mission at Morleyville in 1873. Another contender for first Bow area rancher is whisky-trader-turned-rancher Howell Harris, who brought cattle along when he helped operate a whisky fort on the Highwood River. Harris's cattle were abandoned when local First Nations people ran the traders off; but when Harris returned the following spring, he found most of his cattle had survived the winter—his was the area's first open-range herd.

More traditional cattle ranches started along the Old Man River drainage after the arrival of the Mounties in 1874. Most of those ranches were owned by the mounted policemen, who received land scrip for completing their term of service. A few other Mounties (including Captain Winder) ranched while still in the service of the mounted police.

Fort Macleod, the original mounted police fort, built in 1874, spawned a town of the same name that became the first capital of the Alberta ranch frontier. When the ranch lease legislation came along in 1881, many of the first leases awarded were, again, on the Old Man River drainage. Matthew Cochrane's Cochrane Ranche on the Bow was an

Duncan McEachran was many things in Alberta's frontier ranch era: Canada's veterinary director general; principal purchaser of Canadian re-mounts for the Boer War; and part owner and general manager of two of Alberta's biggest lease ranches. He was also a fierce opponent of squatters.

interesting exception that was probably viewed as ill-advised and eccentric. However, the building of Canada's national railway was about to make Matthew Cochrane seem brilliant; almost clairvoyant.

When the CPR was built in the early 1880s, along a prairie route through Calgary and along the Bow Valley west of Calgary, it was a tremendous boon to Senator Cochrane's ranch. His ranch headquarters were so close to the projected railway line that he would be able to load his beef cattle from his own backyard. The fortuitousness of this is hard to credit as coincidence.

In the summer of 1881, Senator Cochrane came to see his ranch in the company of his resident general manager,

Dr. Duncan McEachran. They travelled by rail through the northern United States to Fort Benton, Montana, and proceeded north by buggy along the Whoop-Up Trail: the old road that had carried a river of whisky into the so-called British Possessions between 1869 and 1874.

Dr. McEachran's name is all over this era of western Canadian history. Besides managing the Cochrane lease, he was also in charge of the giant Walrond Ranch between the Porcupine Hills and Rocky Mountains farther south. He was also Canada's veterinary director general.

When Cochrane and McEachran arrived at the Cochrane lease, they travelled its extent and tried to establish where the boundaries lay. (The land would not be surveyed for some time, and when it was, the ranch would be found to contain 109,000 acres, nine thousand more than the maximum allowed.) What they found on this voyage of discovery was quite a number of squatters, and they proceeded to kick them off. They did not physically remove them, but they promised to do so if they did not leave on their own. One suspects this was more Dr. McEachran's passion than Senator Cochrane's. In the history of his Walrond Ranch (which became known as "the Waldron" through common usage), McEachran conducted a war against squatters, evicting them without payment for improvements, even if the choice to squat on the lease had been accidental.

McEachran conducted a war against squatters, evicting them without payment for improvements, even if the choice to squat on the lease had been accidental.

The Canadian Pacific Railway

In 1871, Prime Minister John A. MacDonald promised British Columbia a railroad within ten years if it would agree to become part of the Canadian Dominion. A scandal over MacDonald's railway scheme caused his government to collapse. When the Conservatives finally returned to power in 1878, the railway still didn't exist and Prime Minister MacDonald had only three years left to fulfill his promise. He turned to private entrepreneurs, and the Canadian Pacific Railway (CPR) was born. A complicated deal with the new company cost Canada much land and money, but construction did begin in 1881.

In its earlier, failed stages, the national railway had favoured a northern route, through Fort Edmonton and over the Rockies by the Yellowhead Pass (in the Jasper area). But when the CPR's route became public, all had changed.

The railway would cross Canada's southern prairies, and the Rocky Mountain crossing would begin in the Bow Valley and climb over the Kicking Horse Pass.

What this abruptly meant was that Fort Macleod could not be the capital of the ranching industry for much longer. Many new leases, after 1881, preferred land near the Bow River and the railway. The Old Man River ranchers understood that they would soon have to trail their beef cattle north to some CPR station along the Bow. The most logical place for this station, this new ranching capital, was the fort and little village of Fort Calgary, which, by luck, was on the new rail line. The change was sudden. Overnight, some stores in Fort Macleod emptied their shelves into wagons and headed north to the new boomtown of Calgary.

The CPR's restored steam train, The Empress, chugs through Glenbow Ranch Provincial Park in 2011. The construction of the CPR mainline reached this part of the Bow Valley in early fall, 1883.

Above: Construction of the Canadian Pacific Railway through Calgary and the Bow Valley meant this stretch of valley was on the path of future development. Ranches, quarries, homesteads, and villages would follow.

Left: The first Canadian Pacific Railway train arrived in Calgary on August 28, 1883.

The Marquis of Lorne
Visits the Cochrane Ranche

The Cochrane Ranche was visited by Canada's Governor General, the Marquis of Lorne, in its first months of existence; in fact, before it had any cows. The marquis was Queen Victoria's son-in-law by virtue of his marriage to Princess Louise Alberta. The name of the province of Alberta (actually of its predecessor, the North West Territories' District of Alberta) was Lorne's idea: a tribute to his wife.

The visit to the Cochrane Ranche took place on September 15, 1881, and was part of Lorne's western tour. He had been on the prairie for about two months when he arrived at the Cochrane Ranche. The marquis was thrilled that he had recently shot his first buffalo, for which he had been searching since he left Winnipeg.

In the year following his western tour, Lorne gave many speeches in praise of the ranching prospects of the West. He told of grass growing to the belly of a tall horse. He described a herd of over six thousand cows that he watched pass near Fort Macleod (the original Cochrane herd on its way north). The Marquis of Lorne was a celebrity, and his praise of the prospects for Alberta ranching had an impact on the upper classes, both in central Canada and in Britain. It may account for the fact that so many lease ranchers in Alberta after 1881 were of the peerage or simply very wealthy. The marquis had made an Alberta ranche a fashionable accoutrement.

Only one squatter successfully called McEachran's bluff, and this man, oddly, had the last name Cochrane. Dave Cochrane was an ex-Mountie who had stayed in southern Alberta, making a living in several usually illegal ways. Bootlegging was one of his mainstays; squatting was another. In the 1870s, he squatted on the future Peigan Reserve, throwing up some quick buildings. When the government came to expropriate the land for the reserve, Cochrane demanded that a tribunal of ranchers assess his loss. This tribunal awarded Dave Cochrane a tidy sum. He tried to repeat the gambit by squatting on the Waldron Lease but was met head on by the implacable Dr. McEachran.

Strange occurrences followed, including a bullet that passed through the Waldron ranch house window. The story is that when McEachran and Cochrane met on their horses one day, Cochrane lit his pipe while listening to McEachran's threats. Holding the lit match aloft, Cochrane mused on how much damage one little match could do if thrown into all this brittle grass. In the end he got his tribunal, but the ranchers were on to him. He was awarded very little money for leaving. In the future, how the Cochrane Ranche dealt with local squatters would have a great deal to do with its Bow River demise.

While Senator Cochrane was viewing his lease, his local manager, James Walker, was in Montana buying the first herds

Left: Colonel James Walker in his North West Mounted Police years (1880). He was one of the original Mounties who rode west from Manitoba in 1874. He left the mounted police to manage the Cochrane Ranche in 1881.

James Walker was chosen as Calgary's "Citizen of the Century" in 1975.

of Cochrane cows. Walker was another former mounted police officer and a respected leader in the Bow Valley's frontier community. He bought cattle in Idaho and in the crowded Beaverhead range of southern Montana. His orders from McEachran were to buy at least six thousand head and to get them onto the Cochrane lease by the first snow. Part of the deal was that the vendors would trail the cattle to the Canadian border. The trail boss put in charge of this drive was Howell Harris, the former whisky trader who claimed to be Alberta's first rancher.

At the border, the herd was handed off to Major Walker, and it was up to him to hire a crew to take them the rest of the way. Several of the cowboys on the first leg signed on to continue the drive to the Bow River ranch. The man chosen as overall boss of the drive was Frank Strong, a foreman for the Circle Ranch, which was owned by Montana businessmen and ranched on both sides of the boundary. Strong divided the herd into "drys" and "wets." The wets were cows with calves. The drys were everything else (dry cows, bulls, steers, and heifers).

Chosen to boss the drys was George Houk, who had been a prospector and whisky trader in western Canada in the 1860s. Jack Allan was in charge of the slower-moving wets. The oral story of what happened next was that the two herds were "tin-canned and slickered" all the way to the Cochrane Ranche.

This meant they were hurried by flapping rain slickers at them and by shaking tins with rocks inside. It amounted to poor care, because the cows were already trail weary. Hurrying them meant that they could not graze along the way and would lose more weight, arriving at the Cochrane in poor condition for winter.

The anecdotal evidence blames the poor management of the herd on everyone from James Walker to Frank Strong to the trail bosses, and the individual drovers, but it was probably the result of orders from Dr. McEachran. It was he who wanted the cattle on the lease before snow, and the cow bosses and cowboys sought only to obey, though it probably went against their instincts. If James Walker did not challenge his boss's orders, it was likely because he was new to ranching.

The cost of hurrying the cows was the loss of many head across the following winter. Some have said it was a bad winter, but the fact is no other Alberta ranchers reported serious losses. The Cochrane loss was 1,500 head, and that did not include calves. (Calves were also not included in the 6,300 tally of the total herd.)

When winter waned and the Cochrane cows began calving, Dr. McEachran ordered that every animal found on the Cochrane lease be branded. Normally, the cattle bought in Montana would have been branded with the big Cochrane "C" the previous summer when they were

When the Cochrane cows began calving, Dr. McEachran ordered that every animal found on the Cochrane lease be branded.

purchased, but there had not been time. They had gone into winter with hair brands, a kind of quick travelling brand where the hair was burned off in the shape of the branding iron. The skin below was not burned and the brand would disappear as the winter hair grew.

The Cochrane branding was a huge affair: weeks of gathering, corralling, and finally branding and castrating. The neighbouring squatters offered their services, but they soon became alarmed. Dr. McEachran's order that every animal on the lease be branded meant that their cattle could also be branded with the "C" if they happened to have wandered onto the unfenced Cochrane lease. One neighbour saw two of his own pet cows driven into a corral. When he asked that his cows be returned to him, the request was denied. They were on Cochrane land and would be branded as Cochrane cattle.

This offended most everyone. The squatters quickly left to search for their cattle. If they thought their cattle had been taken, they took Cochrane Ranche animals as compensation. Some took more than their due, as revenge against the Cochrane's high-handedness. Some Cochrane cowboys also quit. Round-ups on the open range, where no one's cattle were fenced, were often all about returning cattle to rightful owners. To see the opposite principle in force amounted to a form of rustling, and some cowboys would not work for that kind of outfit.

In short, the "brand everything" rule shattered the Cochrane Ranche's reputation just as it was becoming established.

Because the Cochrane Ranche did not yet have enough cattle to fulfil its stocking requirement, James Walker was dispatched to Montana again in the summer of 1882 to buy a second herd. He went back to Montana's Beaverhead range and bargained for a herd of four thousand from the legendary ranching partnership of Philip Poindexter and William Orr. With the deal made and the drive about to begin, Walker received a telegram from McEachran saying he was to break off the deal, because McEachran believed a better deal could be had from the Fort Benton traders, I.G. Baker & Co.

Walker did as he was told, but when he reached Fort Benton, he ran into another McEachran telegram. The I.G. Baker deal was off, and he was ordered to return to the Beaverhead and remake the deal with Poindexter and Orr. When Walker got back to Dillon, the price of the cows had risen by $25,000. Walker bought them anyway but was so troubled by this kind

A view of the Cochrane area and Canadian Pacific Railway tracks, c. 1885.

of dealing that he submitted his resignation to Cochrane and McEachran. He continued on as local manager until a replacement could be found.

When Philip Poindexter approached the Bow River with the new Cochrane Ranche cattle, the herd was hit by a legendary September blizzard that deeply covered the whole of southern Alberta. The new Cochrane herd clustered together in the valley of Fish Creek, and deep snowbanks formed around them. Poindexter sent a messenger to James Walker. He suggested that the best thing for the cattle was to leave them where they were. Let the blizzard end and give them a month to recoup their strength; then drive them slowly home. Walker responded that he wanted the cattle on his lease now. Poindexter did as he was asked, and when he crossed the Bow and met James Walker and the crew that would take the cattle home, the veteran Montana rancher said, "Count them now because tomorrow half of them will be dead."

Though not precisely true, it was a prophetic remark. The management of the Cochrane Ranche had made its earliest mistake over again, and this time their worn-out cattle really were heading into a severe winter. During the winter of 1882–83, the Cochrane may have lost as many as five thousand head of grown cattle, a catastrophic loss by any measure. Worst of all was that many of those cattle need not have died. In the most severe part

of the winter, a Chinook melt had been followed by deep cold causing the snow to form a hard crust. Cattle do not have the ability to paw through hard snow as horses do, and they began to starve. The cattle's instincts were telling them to drift east, beyond the lease boundary, where they would have found uncovered grass. But, compounding earlier errors, the big bosses down east instructed their new manager to keep the Cochrane cattle on the lease no matter what.

If we could stand on the north escarpment of Glenbow Ranch Provincial Park today and look down not only into the valley but through time to the winter of 1882–83, we would see some terrible things. We would see drifting cattle moving east along the river, staggering over the crusted snow, and we would see Cochrane cowboys riding hard to get ahead of those cattle and turn them back to their certain doom. We would see blizzards in which cattle crowded into coulees. We would see family work groups of Siksika people skinning out the frozen carcasses. The skins were for the ranch, the last income that could be gleaned from these sad animals; the payment for the starving Siksika was that they could take the frozen meat.

The result of this terrible winter was that the Cochrane Ranche's management decided to give up trying to ranch cattle on the original Cochrane lease. The Cochranes arranged a second lease farther

W.D. Kerfoot and the British American Ranche

W.D. Kerfoot (left), seen here with his brother Daniel, was placed in charge of the original Cochrane Ranche in 1883, at the point that it changed its name to the British American Ranche.

William D. Kerfoot was born in 1857, in Virginia. As a young man, he worked on ranches in Montana, and in 1883 he came to the Cochrane Ranche looking for a job as a cowboy. He was soon promoted to foreman.

When Matthew Cochrane decided to give up on cattle ranching at the Big Hill location and switched to sheep, he placed Kerfoot in charge. At this point, 1883, the ranch also changed its name, from the Cochrane Ranche to the British American Ranche.

Cochrane and Kerfoot went together to Montana and bought eight thousand Merinos and Shropshires. It was a model drive, averaging six miles a day, and the sheep arrived at the Big Hill "fat as butter." There were various mishaps in the next two years, including a prairie fire that swept the herd, killing some and ruining the wool of others. Still, Kerfoot was able to market lamb to local butchers and to gain a preferred freight rate to send wool to Montreal.

William Kerfoot's major complaint to Matthew Cochrane and his eastern management team was a need for experienced shepherds. Finally, three shepherds were hired from Aberdeen, Scotland, but, not long after they arrived in mid-1886, William Kerfoot was dismissed. Several hundred sheep had gone missing, and the British American Ranche's secretary-treasurer, John M. Browning, held Kerfoot responsible. Denying that responsibility, but also refusing to blame the loss on the shepherd in charge of the flock, resulted in William Kerfoot being fired. Kerfoot immediately sued the British American Ranche to clear his name and was successful. Judge Rouleau of Calgary found Kerfoot's dismissal by the ranch "unreasonable" and awarded Mr. Kerfoot $1,612 in damages. W.D. Kerfoot bought his own ranch in Grand Valley northwest of the town of Cochrane. The Kerfoot family continues to ranch in Grande Valley to this day.

south in the Belly River area. The new lease took the Cochrane Ranche name. In the summer of 1883, the Cochrane cowboys drove the remaining cattle herd south to the new range.

The story of the Cochrane Ranche on the Bow River did not end there, but it altered. The lease still existed and continued to be owned by Matthew Cochrane, but it took on a new name. As the British American Ranche Company, it was managed by W.D. Kerfoot, a Virginian with Montana cattle experience. Kerfoot was instructed to buy sheep, and he brought eight thousand of them from Montana.

The British American Ranche Company's sheep experiment was not a success. In 1888, the part of the original Cochrane lease that lay to the south of the Bow River became the Bow River Horse Ranche, while the part north of the river, the British American Ranche Company, returned to the federal government, which made it available for purchase or homestead in October 1888. Though the land destined to become Glenbow Ranch Provincial Park would continue to be grazed by cattle right to the present day, its time as an open-range ranch had come to a close.

Glenbow Quarry

Left: When the British American Ranche surrendered its lease in 1888, the area was opened to homestead. The Cockbaine family built a log house on the homestead they named the Waverley Ranch.

Right: Joseph and Elizabeth Cockbaine

Horatio Cockbaine

EVEN WITH THE CANADIAN PACIFIC RAILWAY crossing it from end to end, the portion of the Bow Valley that is now Glenbow Ranch Provincial Park was a poor farming prospect as the open-range ranch era gave way to the homestead frontier. A steep-walled arc of cliffs and coulees hemmed and corralled the river terraces, such that private access remained difficult despite the trains that passed through every day. Glenbow Station appeared on the CPR timetable for the first time in 1889, albeit several kilometres east of its eventual location, and that was the origin of the Glenbow name.

Because of the terrain and isolation, dominion surveyors declared this stretch of the Bow Valley's north shore "unfit for cultivation." The area was still attractive enough to lure a few homesteaders after the British American Ranche gave up its lease in 1888. They were not the only homesteaders at Glenbow but Joseph and Elizabeth Cockbaine, an English couple, serve well as exemplars of the homestead era. They arrived at their Glenbow homestead in April 1893, within their first year in Canada. They built a log cabin, and as their family grew, so did their holdings of sheep, horses, and cattle. In winter they piled cattle dung around the walls of their

Mark Cockbaine

house for insulation, and their son, Horatio, travelled the frozen Bow on wooden skates to fetch supplies. For a time, Joseph's brothers, Horatio and Mark, both lived with them.

When Joseph filed for patent on his land, he discovered he had built on the wrong quarter, the northwest of section 30 rather than the northeast. He was given patent to the land and credit for his improvements on the wrong quarter, but that act of charity did not come without censure. "It does seem impossible that any man could be so frightfully stupid," wrote

a land official. The Cockbaines named their ranch Waverley, possibly because Joseph's sister was an avid reader of Sir Walter Scott's novels, *Waverley* being one of Scott's titles.

In 1898, Joseph wrote a letter to the Department of the Interior to complain that he had acquired a neighbour to the west who was fencing his property. "That will cut off our trail to Cochrane and cause us to climb terrible hills to get to the Morley Trail and pass round the Big Hill, and double our distance to Cochrane." He added, "I am shut in by

A rare look into a cowboy's bunkhouse (c. 1900). This was the home of John N. Champion, a ranch hand who worked for the Waverley Ranch.

Bow River and CPR on south, terrible coulees on west, and in fact situated that I shall have to do my shopping in Calgary."

The department wrote back to assure him that his neighbour would have to allow him access to his old trail, but the letter serves to show the physical isolation his family was feeling at Glenbow. By 1901, the Cockbaines had moved on.

Others were willing to give the pretty, inaccessible portion of valley a try. The William F.U. Copeman family replaced the Cockbaines at Waverley Ranch, adding to its size while retaining the name. Frank R. Houghton purchased land in the southern half of section 28, two miles east. But it was the arrival in 1904 of an English

brother and sister—Stephen Christopher Lay Moore and Mary Cresacre Moore— that began the transition of Glenbow from little-wanted grazing property to something quite different: a quarry and a town.

The Moores came from Stratford-upon-Avon where their father was manager and director of the town's largest employer, the Flower and Sons Brewery. Christopher had a classical education that had stopped short of a degree at Oxford. He named their Glenbow area ranch Hertford after his Oxford college. In addition to homesteading a quarter in the northern half of section 28, Moore bought the available surrounding quarters. Besides the promise

An erosion-resistant capstone creates a "hoodoo" as softer surrounding soils are weathered away.

Stephen Christopher Lay Moore, seen here in 1899, came to Glenbow with his sister Mary Cresacre Moore in 1904. On their Hertford Ranch, a significant deposit of high-quality sandstone became the basis of a quarry founded in 1906.

Left: This image of Stephen Avenue, Calgary, in 1912 shows the amount of sandstone employed in the early construction of the city. The fashion had turned to sandstone when a fire destroyed the wooden centre of the nascent city in 1886.

of ranching at this location, Moore's application for homestead noted sandstone formations on the property. Sandstone was the fashionable construction material for elegant homes and public buildings in that era. The sandstone industry had been given an extra push in the District of Alberta after a fire destroyed sixteen businesses in downtown Calgary in 1886. The fire department had sought an ordinance that all downtown buildings be built of sandstone.

In 1906 and early 1907, the sandstone on Christopher Moore's land was already being quarried, and John Gillespie, a Scottish stone mason who was the chief inspector of masonry for the Alberta provincial government's Department of Public Works, came to examine the stone and the operation. In 1907, the quarry changed hands and became the Glenbow Quarry Company, incorporated by officials from the B.C. General Coal Company of Vancouver. George H. Webster was the new company's president and N. Hayden its manager. The concept was to ship stone from Glenbow to British Columbia, but the project soon fell through when closer sources of stone were found.

In 1908, the Moores sold their ranch and moved to Vancouver, where Christopher would work as a secretary for the Canadian Northern Railway Medical Department. When World War I began, he enlisted in the 29th Battalion, Canadian Infantry, which sailed for Britain in May

The Moodie family, pictured here in front of their home at Glenbow in 1892 or '93, was one of the earliest homestead families in what is now Glenbow Ranch Provincial Park.

of 1915. Chris Moore was in a trench in the border area when heavy shelling took place on April 6, 1916. He was badly wounded with broken femurs in both legs, and he died of his wounds in hospital over a month later. He was buried in the same Wimereux cemetery as John McCrae, author of "In Flanders Fields."

The Moores had been able to sell out and move away from Glenbow because of the arrival of two New Yorkers: Leonard H. Kennerley and Chester Rhodes de la Vergne. There is an excellent record of that occasion in the form of a surviving letter from Kennerley to his fiancé, Celia Block. On July 24, 1908, as Leonard sat down in Calgary's Braemar Lodge to write to Celia, he was full of excitement because he and Chester had found exactly what they wanted: beautiful riverside

> Leonard …
> was full of
> excitement
> because he and
> Chester had
> found exactly
> what they
> wanted: beautiful
> riverside ranch-
> land, suitable
> for living, riding,
> hunting, and
> fishing.

ranch-land, suitable for living, riding, hunting, and fishing. The land also contained a potential source of income: a working sandstone quarry. "About a mile away [from the house] is a large stone quarry employing about one hundred men," he wrote.

It is interesting to compare Kennerley's letter, designed to convince his fiancé that she would like to live at Glenbow, to that of Joseph Cockbaine when he was trying to get help with his access problems from the Department of the Interior. While Cockbaine spoke of the terrible hills and the terrible coulees, Leonard Kennerley wrote: "The land is inclined to be hilly at the back but only a very small portion of it, the rest of the land being flat with occasional gullies running through it. Running right through the property is a splendid stream of water fed entirely by springs."

The proposed partnership between de la Vergne and Kennerley was described in the letter as "in every way satisfactory." Leonard declared himself "absolutely sure of its ultimate success. Chester himself has absolute faith in the land as a speculation." As for the house on the Moore property, it was built of "four thicknesses of timber" and was so satisfactory that "even Chester said he would be perfectly contented to live in it."

Another letter from Leonard to Celia, dated August 14, 1908, declared that the deal was done. Chester and Leonard had

taken over immediate possession of 343 acres (138.8 hectares), its buildings, household effects, and animals. By January 1909, they would have another 1,520 acres (615 hectares) and a second house and buildings.

In this letter, Leonard left a description of the view from their new property. "The Rockies are to be seen from both houses. In all kinds of weather they look magnificent, some days looking at them one can imagine that the whole range of mountains is unreal they look so far away and again at times they look very close and appear almost human in their grandeur. I think I could write forever of the charms of this beautiful section of the country but I must leave you a chance to see these wonderful sights for yourself firsthand."

It was while Chester de la Vergne and Leonard Kennerley were staying in Braemar Lodge, Calgary, that Kennerley wrote to his fiancé, Celia Block, to praise the property de la Vergne had purchased at Glenbow that day in 1908.

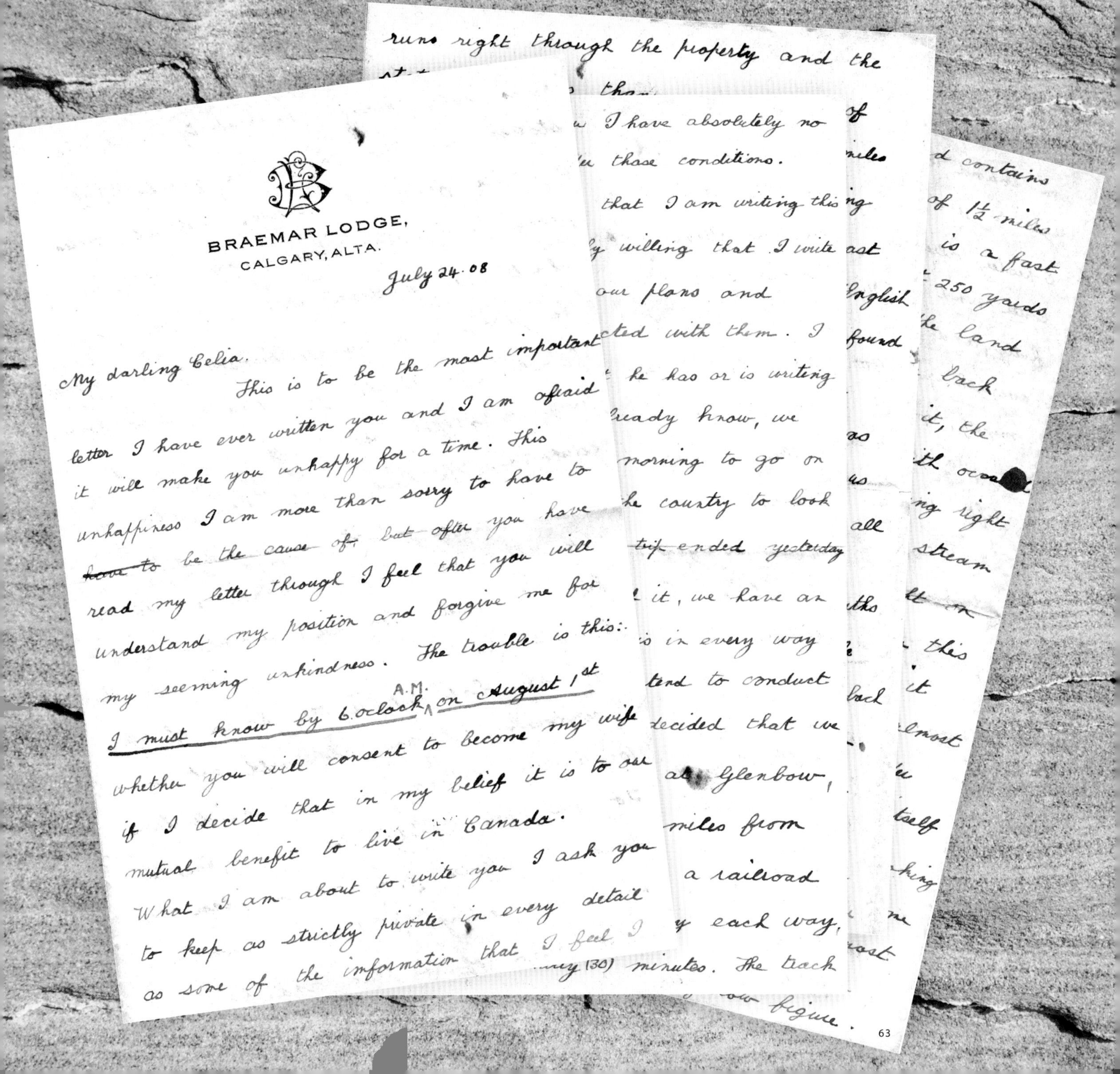

BRAEMAR LODGE,
CALGARY, ALTA.

July 24·08

My darling Celia,

　　　This is to be the most important letter I have ever written you and I am afraid it will make you unhappy for a time. This unhappiness I am more than sorry to have to ~~have~~ be the cause of, but after you have read my letter through I feel that you will understand my position and forgive me for my seeming unkindness. The trouble is this:‑

I must know by 6 o'clock A.M. on August 1st whether you will consent to become my wife if I decide that in my belief it is to our mutual benefit to live in Canada.

What I am about to write you I ask you to keep as strictly private in every detail as some of the information that I feel I

[second page — partially obscured]

runs right through the property and the
...
... I have absolutely no ...
... these conditions.
... that I am writing this ...
... willing that I write ...
... our plans and ... English
... with them. I found
... he has or is writing
... ready know, we
... morning to go on
... the country to look
... trip ended yesterday
... it, we have an ...
... in every way
... tend to conduct
... decided that we
... at Glenbow,
... miles from
... a railroad
... each way,
...(30) minutes. The track
... figure.

[third page — partially obscured]

... contains
... of 1½ miles
... is a fast
... 250 yards
... the land
... back
... it, the
... with ...
... right
... stream
...
... this
... it
... most
...
... itself
...
...

Chester de la Vergne and his manager Leonard Kennerley stand in front of the Moore house after de la Vergne bought the Hertford Ranch in 1908. The Moore house remains in Glenbow Ranch Provincial Park to this day.

The connection between Kennerley and de la Vergne was that Kennerley's fiancé Celia was the sister of Chester's wife, Gladys. The women were daughters of Louis Block, who was Chester de la Vergne's father's business partner. De la Vergne Senior and Block had made a fortune in the refrigeration business, creating the world's first refrigerated rail cars, capable of bringing California produce to the cities of the east.

The de la Vergnes' arrival in January 1909 and their approach to living on the frontier give an idea of the standard of living the family was used to. Chester may have declared himself content to live in the house at Glenbow, but Gladys wanted no part of it. She and the de la Vergne children, Chester and Gertrude, remained living at the Braemar Lodge in Calgary until a new house was built for them.

Chapman Bros. from Cochrane got the contract for the new de la Vergne house, which was built high on one of the coulees. The new house was to have running water, two bathrooms, and electricity. Two wells were witched and dug to great depth. Furnishings for the home came from New York City in a rail car. Also arriving were a Percheron stallion, an Irish hunter, hunting dogs, a cook, two English maids, a governess, and a nurse.

The Kennerleys' home (formerly the Moore house) was nearby. Both homes had stables. At de la Vergne's, besides the thirteen-horse stable, there was a separate building for Gracieux, their Percheron stallion.

"It is a wonderful sight to see the cranes running overhead on heavy walls of timbers, lifting up easily and simply a stone weighing over twenty tons at a time."

One of the most striking elements of the story of Glenbow is how suddenly things happened in 1909. Within that year, Chester de la Vergne stocked his ranch with sheep, cattle, Percherons, and polo ponies, and saw the completion of his new house. Meanwhile at the quarry site, a new company had taken over. The Glenbow Quarry Company had sold the operation to the Alberta government in 1908, and, in 1909, the Quinlan and Carter Quarry Company had won the government tender and had hired masons and stoneworkers from Scotland to get it rolling again. Seeing the potential for a town, Chester de la Vergne had a townsite surveyed and dragged an old farmhouse (the Fitzgerald house) across the railway track to serve as a post office and general store. The community built a race track and a polo ground, and staged a fall race meet.

In all this furious development, the one feature of Glenbow that was experiencing delay was its bridge. For the town to succeed, a bridge was needed across the Bow River to the south bank. In his July 24, 1908, letter to Celia, Leonard Kennerley was already commenting on this need but, well into 1909, the bridge project was still no more than a petition to the provincial government. The most promising news was that local politician C.W. Fisher had promised the bridge as part of his campaign for re-election to the provincial legislature.

Another nuisance was the mail. A local citizen described the problem this way: "Our mail bags are being carried past in the morning on [train] No. 97, are left in Cochrane all day long and fetched back at midnight on the No. 96." This was not commensurate with Glenbow's growth, which was expected to eclipse that of Cochrane.

Through 1909, the Glenbow quarry turned out immense amounts of sandstone. The *Cochrane Advocate*, though often annoyed by Glenbow's boosterism, openly admired its quarry. "It is a wonderful sight to see the cranes running overhead on heavy walls of timbers, lifting up easily and simply a stone weighing over twenty tons at a time. The works all through are complete and strictly first class in every shape and form. Over one hundred men are working now in the works."

By 1903, the Glenbow CPR station had moved to its final position a mile west of the quarry. In 1908, a new siding called Impey was added below the quarry, to facilitate the transportation of the stone.

John Quinlan, president of the Quinlan and Carter Quarry Company, was from Montreal: a "blasphemous Irishman" by one account. William J. Carter, the vice-president, was an Ontario man who had begun his career in contracting in the fledgling town of Prince Albert in 1879. During the Métis Resistance of 1885, Carter had played an active role on the Canadian government side. He moved to

The state of the art equipment for the quarry included diamond saws, flat and cornice planers, and a five-hundred-horsepower engine.

Calgary, then to central Canada, and back west to Edmonton, where his partnership with John Quinlan began. The Alberta Legislature in Edmonton was under construction at the time, and the Quinlan and Carter Quarry Company secured the contract to supply it with Glenbow sandstone. Stone quarried and planed at the Glenbow quarry became part of other Alberta public buildings, such as Calgary's new courthouse and its land titles building.

The state of the art equipment for the quarry included diamond saws, flat and cornice planers, and a five-hundred-horsepower engine. Tools were made on site by men trained in Scotland. The stone was near the top of the cliff, and, once quarried, it was lowered to a level halfway down for cutting and planing. A final lowering brought it to the level of the railway where it was loaded onto flatcars. During its peak period, two twelve-hour shifts kept the quarry at work around the clock.

The most spectacular incident in the quarry's early life had to do with lowering stone between the levels. The system that Mr. Quinlan inherited from Mr. Hayden featured two sets of vertical rail tracks. A long cable lowered a car on one track while the weight pulled an empty car up the other track. A wheel with a brake controlled the descent and bore the strain. When John Quinlan saw this contraption, he was convinced it would fail. He replaced it with a proper winch and drum, weighing

several tons. When the winch was installed on the steep hillside, a great deal of rock was piled in front to prevent its being pulled down.

In an interview that took place decades later, Tom Wearmouth, a quarryman whose family stayed in the Cochrane district, told a harrowing story about the new winching system's debut. Tom was operating the winch on a trial run when the cable came off the drum. Because no stones were piled on the timbers behind the drum, the entire mechanism somersaulted forward over the retaining rocks. It fell into the quarry. The carload of stone that was being lowered at the time ran wild and snapped the winch out of the quarry. At "express-train speed" the car, dragging the winch, sped through the sheds below. The cable broke; the car spilled its load of rocks then vaulted the CPR tracks. Winch and car came to final rest, "both badly wrecked."

Amazingly, no one was killed. The previous system for lowering the stone was reinstalled.

The prediction in the spring of 1909 was that accommodation would be needed for 150 quarrymen and eighty stonecutters. That year, Chester de la Vergne hired a Calgary company to survey land north and south of the CPR into residential lots. A triangular area on a bench south of the rail line became the quarry workers' village, and the area north of the CPR was

Sandstone from the Glenbow Quarry was used in the construction of Alberta'a Legislative Building in Edmonton.

never developed. Beyond selling lots, Mr. de la Vergne did not seem to take much responsibility for the village of Glenbow. His cattle grazed around the shacks of the village, and one of his cows spent a good part of the summer with a pillowcase on her horns after a run-in with a clothesline. When Joe Towell wrote a letter of complaint, Chester de la Vergne told him to build a fence and put an end to the nuisance.

An indication of the population at Glenbow in 1909 was the amount of business done at the general store.

When the Fitzgerald house was dragged across the tracks and opened as a store, proprietor Sandi McDonald was immediately busy. Two days after opening day, April 29, 1909, he reported that forty-three people were in his store at once.

There were a surprising number of entertainments available in the community of Glenbow. During the open-range ranch era, the sport of polo had been introduced to the region by the ranching set and was quickly adopted by cowboys and anyone else with a passion for horses. At Glenbow, on weekends,

Left: Stone masons worked with Glenbow sandstone in the creation of Alberta's Parliament Building in the period after 1905.

the local polo team would either play on the Glenbow field or away in Cochrane and Millarville.

The higher wage earners at the quarry built a Stonecutters' Hall where dances were held every Saturday night. The stonecutters bought an organ for the hall that would eventually be donated to Glenbow's school. Storekeeper Sandi McDonald assembled a citizen's band. During the summer, the quarrymen staged picnics on a little island in the Bow, where there were races and contests.

The biggest entertainment of 1909 was probably Glenbow's September race meet. Race day was September 10, and the CPR put on a special train from Calgary. Nine races were scheduled. The prizes were mainly cash, but there was a "Lady's Bracelet" awarded to the winner of the Open Race for geldings and mares. Local ranchers, the Payn le Sueur brothers, were famous for their horses, and each won a race. The day was slightly marred when, in the final event, a steeplechase, a Calgary horse, Kingsford Kid, ran into a post and broke his back, dying instantly. The *Cochrane Advocate* reported:"The rider was injured about the head and face and was taken to Calgary on a freight train for surgical treatment."

If the story of Glenbow stopped right here, at the end of its first race meet and with the quarry humming around the clock, who could have guessed what the

future would hold? It was not that far-fetched a forecast that the hopes of Glenbow's boosters would come true. In the summer of 1909, in the *Calgary Herald*, one such booster wrote that Glenbow "was destined to become a large town in the course of very few years. It is beautifully situated for early spring market gardening as well as for a health resort and residential purposes. Not even our foes can despise us."

This kind of talk was sometimes a bit more than the nearby town of Cochrane could tolerate. The *Cochrane Advocate* shot back, "One of these days the *Herald* will wake up to the fact that it is being fooled. Several race meetings, we learn, are being arranged for in that metropolis [Glenbow] for this season. A further item

One of the worker's shacks below the Glenbow Quarry (c. 1910). Most of the single workers lived in a large bunkhouse.

Glenbow Sandstone

The sandstone at Glenbow is from the Porcupine Hills Formation. Between sixty-eight and fifty-five million years ago, sand eroded from the ancestral Rocky Mountains was transported to the Calgary area by ancient rivers. Minerals in the groundwater cemented the sand into stone that was later exposed by the carving of the modern river channel. At the turn of the twentieth century, when sandstone was a popular construction material for public buildings, the exposed sandstone from Calgary to Cochrane was examined for quality. At Calgary, the sandstone was yellowish-buff; at Cochrane, it was grey; and, in between, at Glenbow, the stone was an attractive yellowish-buff to yellowish-grey. The Glenbow sandstone was also soft and easily worked.

The sandstone quarry at Glenbow ran between 1906 and 1912. By the latter date, the best of the sandstone was gone and the rest could not compete with faraway quarries.

This photo shows a grain elevator under construction in Alberta. In the *Cochrane Advocate*, Chester de la Vergne's Glenbow grain elevator was described as follows: "The elevator, built by C.E. Benell of Brandon, has a capacity of 30,000 bushels, and is operated by a 10 h.p. Otto gasoline engine … Farmers' wagons drive in from one side on to a Fairbanks/ scale, which weighs up to 12,000 lbs, and having dumped their load into a bin beneath the scale, pass out the other side."

of poignant interest informs Calgary that 'several gophers have been killed, showing signs of an early spring.' Things must be pretty slow in the Elevator City when occasional deaths among the gophers are matters of comment."

The elevator referred to in the above newspaper piece was a grain elevator that Chester de la Vergne was planning to build beside the railway track at Glenbow, as soon as the bridge across the Bow was underway. He had already decided that the north–south boundary between sections 28 and 29 would be a street, and its name would be "Bridge Street."

The one thing that almost no one could have predicted for Glenbow was what actually happened, and that is the subject of the next essay.

Millionaire Hill
and Glenbow Village

IN ITS HEYDAY, THE VILLAGE OF GLENBOW had a highly visible social stratification. There was a village in the valley below the quarry for the quarry workers and their families. There was a large bunkhouse, mostly for bachelor quarrymen. On the hill to the north, the de la Vergnes and three other well-to-do families lived in handsome homes that went by the collective nickname "Millionaire Hill." Some contend these families were less than actual millionaires, and, given that a million 1910 dollars is equivalent to twenty-three million 2010 dollars, perhaps not. But they were certainly wealthy enough to command a life-style most would envy.

While the people in the village, Glenbow proper, worked hard at their industrial jobs and at keeping their modest homes, the well-to-do on Millionaire Hill had, to outward appearances, grand lives of relative ease. They had staffs of servants; they raced, hunted, travelled,

Chester de la Vergne's homesite and ranch buildings. His was the first of four grand homes along Millionaire Hill above the townsite of Glenbow.

> Most of the well-to-do group were from New York and were either moving away or taking a break from the urban world.

and held grand parties. If the quality British soap-opera *Upstairs, Downstairs* were ever adapted to the history of Glenbow, a good title would be *Uphill, Downhill,* for the stories of Glenbow tend to focus on the lives above and the lives below, plus the commercial and social interactions and intrigues between.

The people who lived downhill in Glenbow were, for the most part, working families who were there for the quarry. Those living uphill had little to do with the industrial side of the settlement. Most of the well-to-do group were from New York and were either moving away or taking a break from the urban world. What they hoped to achieve at Glenbow was a mixture of sanctuary, recuperation, freedom, and adventure. Some wanted to hunt and ride in the wilds; some wanted to fly airplanes.

For the wealthy at Glenbow, the de la Vergnes had set a template. Their home, built in 1909, was "comfortably set at the top of a coulee," according to a description in the *Cochrane Advocate* in 1910. The article described the residence as "large and comfortable and fitted well with all modern conveniences."

By contemporary standards, the de la Vergne house was not enormous. A 1920 description, written on Palliser Hotel stationary (perhaps written by Chester de la Vergne himself), stated that its ground dimensions were thirty-two by forty-two

feet, which tallies with Cochrane builder William Chapman's 1909 contract to excavate a thirty- by forty-foot basement. Across the west side of the house was a full-length enclosed veranda, taking good advantage of the view of the Rockies. There were ten rooms in the two storeys, plus an attic and a full masonry basement eight feet deep. The house had steam heat, two bathrooms, and running water. Behind it were a "scientifically built" ice house, a workshop, and an engine room.

The 1920 description mentioned a six-room "manager's cottage," close to the de la Vergne house. This was probably the

Leonard Kennerley, seen here with his first child, moved from Glenbow to Calgary, where he became involved in the development and sale of real estate.

Christopher Moore house, into which Leonard Kennerley moved with his new wife in late 1909. There are mysteries involving the Kennerley–de la Vergne relationship. The business partnership between Chester and Leonard, which sounded so positive in 1908, came apart in 1910. The Kennerleys left Glenbow and moved to Calgary, where Leonard became involved in real estate. Celia purchased one of Leonard's riverside lots in the Bowness area on which they built themselves a comfortable bungalow.

Among the first arrivals to Glenbow from New York were John Hallett Clark and his wife Sarah, who came to the valley in 1910. The Clarks chose to live in the lower valley rather than on the hill, as their goal was to run a working ranch. They bought the Waverley Ranch, which had changed hands a few times since the Cockbaine family homesteaded there and provided its name. John Clark's career had been with the New York Stock Exchange, and, because of this experience, and probably because of his age (forty-seven), Chester de la Vergne suggested he seek work with the Calgary Grain Exchange. Instead, the Clarks pursued ranching, bringing the first Holstein cows to the area and purchasing one of the first tractors.

The Clarks became close friends with their neighbours, the Tom James family, who had immigrated from Bristol, England, in 1905. Tom and Annie James were homesteaders and had six children.

When the Clarks arrived in 1910, the James boys were working at the quarry. Tom James would become an early threshing machine operator: part of a team that threshed grain for local farmers on contract. Clark's ranch foreman, Alex Milne, was a Scot who was good with horses. Milne enjoyed whisky and, when he ran out, would go to the general store for Worcester Sauce, which he drank straight from the bottle.

The next New Yorkers to build at Glenbow did so on a hilltop not far from de la Vergne's. They were C.F.R. (Craig) Drake and his wife Mary, who was one of Chester de la Vergne's two sisters. The Drakes bought a quarter-section west of the de la Vergne's house, and Craig Drake, being an architect, designed their grand

John and Sarah Clark of New York bought the Waverley Ranch. Seen here with their neighbours and friends, the Tom James family from England. L to R: Sissie James, Elsie James, Mrs. John H. Clark, Mrs. Tom James, John H. Clark, Tom James.

Left: Major George Edmond de St. Clair Stevenson. The major and his wife Kathleen built their Glenbow home on Millionaire Hill after the Drake and Morris families built theirs.

The Stevenson house was built while Major Stevenson was on medical leave from the British army. He returned to England at the commencement of World War I. The sandstone first storey of the Stevenson house remains today: a dramatic ruin overlooking the park and the valley.

home. He personally selected every important piece of wood in it. The Drakes called their property the Buckspring Ranch, and their intention was to live half the year at Glenbow and half in New York.

Friends of the Drakes, Dr. and Mrs. D.H. Morris, also of New York, followed soon after. The Morris family built on the quarter immediately south of Buckspring Ranch. That Dr. Dudley Morris had served as an usher at the New York wedding of Chester's sister Katherine to Archibald Ewing Stevenson suggests there was a prior friendship with the de la Vergnes that contributed to the move. The Morris's Glenbow home was similar in scale to the Drakes' (both contained thirty rooms). The large fireplaces at either end of the Morris house were made of stones that Currey Wearmouth of Glenbow

Dr. Dudley Henry Morris and Gertrude Powell were New York friends of the Drake family who built their Glenbow home directly south of Buckspring Ranch. They are pictured here on their wedding day in 1910.

village gathered from the river edge. Dr. Morris had assigned Currey to find rocks that were liberally decorated with lichen.

Dudley Henry Morris was a medical doctor, and the son of a doctor. He was a Yale graduate who had joined the College of Physicians in New York and became the head of Emergency at Columbia Presbyterian Hospital in New York City. The move to Glenbow was spurred by Dr. Morris's asthma. His physician had told him that he needed a dry climate, maybe Arizona, but he chose Alberta instead. Morris acquired the paperwork necessary to practice medicine in Alberta and travelled to his patients in a buggy drawn by a handsome team of chestnut horses.

The last of the Millionaire Hill set who would build on the hill were the Stevensons: Major George Edmond de St. Clair Stevenson and his wife Kathleen. The fact that Chester de la Vergne had a sister named Katherine whose married name was Stevenson led over time to the perception that the Millionaire Hill Stevensons were de la Vergne's sister and brother-in-law. In fact, Katherine de la Vergne was married to Archibald Ewing Stevenson of New York. Though they probably visited Glenbow, they did not have a house there. George Edmond de St. Clair Stevenson, the name on the Glenbow land title, was a major in the British army. His wife Kathleen was from the wealthy New York Coddington family.

When George and Kathleen Stevenson

The move to Glenbow was spurred by Dr. Morris's asthma. His physician had told him that he needed a dry climate, maybe Arizona, but he chose Alberta instead.

77

Gertrude de la Vergne, daughter of Chester and Gertrude, became Alberta's first female pilot.

While living at Glenbow, Dr. Morris provided much-needed medical service to local residents. In the winter, he travelled by horse-drawn sled.

arrived in Glenbow, they built on Millionaire Hill between the de la Vergnes and the Drakes. It is said that the major was on sick leave from the British army, having punctured a lung in a riding accident. The grandeur of their home is suggested by a first storey made of sandstone (quarried on site) and the fact that there were seven fireplaces. Strong evidence that the Millionaire Hill group were all friends was a telephone line that connected the four homes.

What life was like on Millionaire Hill can be gleaned in various ways. Chester de la Vergne may have been the only active polo player among them, but attending the games at Glenbow, plus the away matches, would have been recreation for all. The de la Vergnes were all avid riders. Mrs. de la Vergne rode side-saddle even when jumping in competition. The de la Vergne family entered various classes at the Calgary Horse Show each spring and daughter, Gertrude, took many

Above: Katherine de La Vergne, (2nd from right) and friends, 1905.

The Bearspaw Families

Both across the Bow River and downstream from Glenbow lived a ranching community that pre-dated the Glenbow quarry and village. The buildings of the Bow River Horse Ranche are still visible from Glenbow Ranch Provincial Park. For many years, they were in use as a Western movie set. Gilbert E. Goddard started with this ranch as its bookkeeper in 1888 and became manager in 1890. Together with the Warner brothers of England, he purchased the ranch in 1893, and was still resident and in charge during the Glenbow era. The families of Millionaire Hill often crossed the river to visit.

On the north side of the river, and downstream from Glenbow, the three Rawlinson brothers were the first to ranch in the Bearspaw District. The Cambridge-educated brothers specialized in Hackney horses and sold 155 of them in 1907 at a dispersal sale that drew buyers from all over the continent.

Another prominent horse family were the Payn le Sueur brothers who leased the original Glenbow Ranch from 1907 to 1911. Harold and Edward Payn le Sueur played on the Glenbow polo team, and they both won races at the Glenbow race meet of 1909. Around this time, the Glenbow Ranch changed its name to Bearspaw Ranch. The family in residence was the "Condie" Landales. Landale was an ex-British army major, and he and his family were devoted to horses, riding, and polo.

Condie Landale (3rd from left) playing polo, c. 1902, when his family lived at Bearspaw Ranch.

firsts. Their long rides at Glenbow often featured picnics, and they rode as far as Banff to overnight. Later, there were automobile excursions. Gertrude de la Vergne took up flying, becoming Alberta's first female pilot.

The lives of the uphill and downhill people were, needless to say, different. In 1910 and 1911, when the wealthy set were arriving and building, the quarry was still running double shifts and turning out stone. Glenbow village had acquired quite a few inhabitants. Among them were Currey and Betty Wearmouth, and most of what we know today about the early village comes from Betty Wearmouth's recollections (as published in the local history *Taming the Prairie Wool*). The Wearmouths were from Durham, England, and Currey and two of his brothers, Tom and George, worked at Glenbow's quarry at the same time.

Betty Wearmouth remembered that there were sixteen shacks and several tents in Glenbow when she and Currey lived in the workers' village. The first purpose of the village was to accommodate quarrymen who had wives and children. For example, the Hugh McLean family had six children and the Lambie family four. But there were bachelors in the village, too. Several of these paid rent in a log house built and owned by Tom Minn. Minn, a Cockney, with experience as a horse-drawn cab driver in the Bowery district of New York City, managed Chester de la Vergne's stables. Some of the Glenbow bachelors took their meals at Mrs. Towell's shack. Another quarryman's wife, Mrs. Sid Scott, took in laundry.

In Glenbow, one supposes there were all sorts of dealings like these, ways people thought up to get ahead. Cecil Edwards, who took over the general store from Sandi McDonald, hired a German to drive a buggy to the village, taking orders and making deliveries. A few quarry workers homesteaded locally, using their quarry wages to pay the costs of "proving up" and acquiring patent on their land. Tom Wearmouth was one of these, riding back and forth between the quarry and his farm. Homesteaders Tom Norris and his son Sid found a different way to combine farming with work at Glenbow. They did not work for the quarry nor live at Glenbow but were carpenters who built several town buildings. Currey and Betty Wearmouth's shack was one of their projects, as was Glenbow School, built in 1911–12.

Defining these two groups, wealthy and working class, uphill and down, makes them sound like two solitudes, but, within the conventions of class difference, there were many kinds of interaction. Merely by coming to Glenbow and having houses built there, the New Yorkers spurred the local economy and involved the growing

Right: The Glenbow School was built in 1912 by local farmer/carpenter Tom Norris and his sons.

Below: Miss Olive Orr's class from Glenbow School, c. 1912-13.

Another type of interaction was romance. The downhill bachelors and the female servants in the uphill homes were bound to notice each other.

community. The de la Vergnes tried to buy most of their supplies at the Glenbow general store, and, quite likely, the other New Yorkers followed suit. There was also a butcher who came to Glenbow from Calgary: another business that would have been patronized by uphill folks and down.

The interest of the wealthy families in the life and fate of Glenbow is also visible in the records of Glenbow School. When the Norris-built school was ready for students in the spring of 1912, the Honourable C.W. Fisher came to present a flag, and Mrs. Sarah Clark officially opened the school. In the early years, Chester de la Vergne, Craig Drake, and George Stevenson were among those who filled the school trustee and secretary-treasurer positions.

Another type of interaction was romance. The downhill bachelors and the female servants in the uphill homes were bound to notice each other. When these girls were heard to complain of boredom, men from the quarry started dances at Glendale School, a venue more accessible to the servant women than the quarry bunkhouse or Stonecutters Hall where the downhill dances took place. In summer, when the quarrymen hosted picnics on a near-shore island in the Bow River, the families from Millionaire Hill brought their servants down for the occasion.

A noteworthy uphill-downhill romance saw Tom Gillard, a stone-loader at the quarry, marry Ethel Hughes, the de la

Vergne's governess. Betty Wearmouth's account of the wedding in *Taming the Prairie Wool*, states that, "Everyone around attended the wedding, except the best man." The best man, Tom Wearmouth, did not make it.

The present and future of Glenbow changed abruptly and forever in 1912. That year, the Quinlan and Carter quarry closed. The cause was likely a change in the quality of the sandstone. When the quarry at Glenbow began, the stone was an ideal yellow-buff of workable hardness. As they dug more deeply into the cliff, the stone became a less desirable kind called "blue hardhead." When the quarry was not turning out enough good stone, they brought in Ohio stone that was a close colour match. The stonecutters and planers at Glenbow viewed the Ohio stone as "scab-cut stone" and would not touch it. They went on strike. All these reasons added up to the closure.

For Chester de la Vergne, the shutting down of the quarry was half of a one-two punch. The second blow was that the Alberta government did not follow through on C.W. Fisher's promise to build the bridge. De la Vergne's grain elevator was an instant dud that would never have more than a few hundred bushels inside it.

When the quarry closed, the writing was on the wall for most of the population of Glenbow. People had no choice but to move. The families of industrial workers like miners and quarrymen may have dreamt that each new place they moved to was a permanent home, but the more dependable scenario was that economic downturns and other kinds of collapse and change sent them packing over and over. Betty and Currey Wearmouth watched their neighbours depart. The McKechnies returned to Scotland; the McLeans went to Prince Edward Island. Soon most of the shacks of the village were deserted.

The quarrymen who doubled as homesteaders did not have to leave the country, but they now faced the pressure of living by farming alone. One of these, Richard Coxon, bought the Stonecutters' Hall and dragged it up from Glenbow to his farm as an out-building. John Birchall was another who worked for the quarry but stayed in the area afterward. Walter Gooding, who was already established on his homestead and was a handy carpenter, wrecked one of the Glenbow homes and took the wood home to build an extension to his house. Many of these families have descendents in the Cochrane area to this day.

The last hope for the town was a stiff-mud brick plant that started up after the quarry's closure. Twenty acres of clay land, north of the CPR line and east of the general store, were purchased by the brick-making company. The plant was constructed and a short railway spur line served it. The norm for brick-making in western Canada at the time was to press the clay into steel moulds. The stiff-mud process was a bit more exotic in that a column of clay was pushed through a tapered opening then cut into bricks with a wire. At its peak, the brickworks

This hazy view of Glenbow is the only photo in existence that shows the town, c. 1927.

turned out fifty thousand bricks a day. Unfortunately, the bricks, like Glenbow's sandstone, were not up to the standards of competition, and this venture went into debt and closed.

Without the bridge, without the quarry, without the brickworks, the only work left at Glenbow was on the de la Vergne ranch, or building homes on Millionaire Hill. Working on the Morris and Drake homes was how Currey Wearmouth kept his family in Glenbow. Two bachelor carpenters, Peter Bertram and Jack Ross, occupied one of the empty Glenbow shacks while working on the Morris house and the Stevenson barn. Farmer Walter

Gooding and his brother Frank also worked on the Morris house, and Walter and his wife Clara sold milk and butter from their farm to Mr. Edwards at the store.

Since the quarry was not the reason why the New Yorkers came to Glenbow, its closure did not trigger their departure. The outbreak of World War I seemed to be the spark for the first exodus from Millionaire Hill. In 1914, the Stevensons left. About the same time, Dr. Morris decided that he must return to the US for reasons related to the war, though his country was not among the combatants. Contributing to Mr. Morris's reasoning was that he had been having little luck collecting his doctor fees from local patients. A day spent knocking on doors, with a total gross of $7.00, has been cited as a final straw.

Not all the servants of the Morris and Stevenson households left with them. Mary Short, the Stevenson's cook, bought the McLean shack at Glenbow and did laundry there. Every few days, the de la Vergne children, Gertrude and Chester,

> The bounteous food for these parties was seldom eaten, and Mrs. Vanderhoof would put on an open house next day for the locals.

could be seen walking down the hill to Mrs. Short's carrying a laundry basket, one child on each handle.

A morale booster after the various defeats and departures was the 1914 arrival from New York of Mrs. Gertrude Vanderhoof and her twelve-year-old daughter, also named Gertrude. Mrs. Vanderhoof was an old friend of the Stevensons and had visited them in Glenbow. Now she planned to rent their house for two years. Mrs. Vanderhoof was very wealthy. She had married Mr. Vanderhoof on his deathbed: strictly a marriage of convenience to convey part of his considerable funds into her name. When, miraculously, Mr. Vanderhoof recovered, the couple lived together for a year then separated. During that year, their daughter Gertrude was born.

At Glenbow, Mrs. Vanderhoof continued her lavish lifestyle. She brought with her a considerable staff: a male secretary, a governess (Miss Slack), a cook (Mrs. Mole), and a maid (Jenny Johnson). Two local men, Currey Wearmouth and George Anderson, went to work for her as a groom and handyman. Prior to this, Anderson had worked for the Payn le Sueur brothers as a horse trainer and for Condie Landale.

Like the de la Vergnes, Mrs. Vanderhoof showed at the Calgary Horse Show. George Anderson, an expert in the art of grooming, prepared her high-stepping pony, Baby Johnny, for the show.

At home in Glenbow, Mrs. Vanderhoof became famous for her lavish parties. One that became local legend was a so-called "Negro Party." From *Taming the Prairie Wool* comes this excellent description:

Currey and George brought in cobwebs from the barn to put around the room. Carrots in bunches hung from nails, paper patches were glued on the windows, and a dog was tied in one corner and a rooster in the other. A hitching rail was put up outside to be used instead of the barn. Currey was made black for the occasion and wore a large yellow sash around his waist, and he took the horses from the guests as they arrived. Mrs. Mole cooked huge quantities of food, and they were served on three large silver trays.

The bounteous food for these parties was seldom eaten, and Mrs. Vanderhoof would put on an open house next day for the locals. She would receive until everyone had arrived, then would leave the maids to entertain and serve.

This receipt recovered from the Glenbow Store and Post Office building, dates to 1917, and documents the purchase by Glenbow Supply Company of goods from the John Irwin Co. Ltd. for Mrs. Vanderhoff. Groceries listed include angelica, basket tomatoes, head lettuce, plums, celery, grapes, cucumber, melons, and hubbard squash.

Mr. and Mrs. Cecil Edwards in the doorway of their general store and post office.

The after-flourish that Gertrude Vanderhoof brought to Glenbow was never meant to last. When she and her daughter left in 1916, the fact had to be faced that Glenbow was unlikely to rise again. A portent had come the year prior when the grain elevator burned down. It not only burned but fell over the railway tracks while on fire, stopping trains for a full twenty-four hours.

The Drakes followed their friends back to New York, and even Currey and Betty Wearmouth, who had stayed through thick and thin, departed. They were invited to do so by Chester de la Vergne, who had bought a section of land a few miles northwest of Millionaire Hill and needed someone to live there to prevent his having to pay extra taxes. Their move took place in 1916.

A footnote to Mrs. Vanderhoof's departure is that her groom George Anderson and her maid Jenny Johnson were married. Jenny was a high-spirited joking type who once dressed up in one of Mrs. Vanderhoof's gowns and wore it to a dance with George. Mrs. Vanderhoof was not present at the event, and the story does not include whether she ever found out. Another trick Jenny liked to play was to *over*-warm Mrs. V's chamber pot.

One of the biggest milestones in Glenbow history was the day, in 1918, that the de la Vergne family moved from their ranch. They did not go far, only to Calgary where Chester entered the car business,

selling Hudson-Essex automobiles. To run the ranch in his absence, Chester hired Dick Widger. In 1922, Widger leased the ranch, and de la Vergne took another step away.

With most of the village deserted, and with the de la Vergnes and the other "millionaires" gone, Glenbow was a much diminished place. Deprived of their best customer, Cecil and Jessie Edwards closed Glenbow's general store. The decline in Glenbow can be read in the Henderson Directory's statistics. In 1911, the population was 350; in 1914, it was fifty.

By the 1920s, only a couple of families remained. Currey and Betty Wearmouth were one of these families, having returned to Glenbow after their stint at the de la Vergne's northern section. Their family and another prompted the reopening of Glenbow school in 1922. It would stay open until 1928 and then close for good. The last of the New Yorkers at Glenbow proved to be the Clarks, John Hallett and Sarah, at the Waverley Ranch. Showing the interest in the school that his own family and the other New Yorkers always had, John Clark was trustee and secretary-treasurer of Glenbow School during its 1922–28 revival. Someone put an end to his trusteeship by pointing out that an American national was ineligible, but he went on as secretary-treasurer to the end. Sadly, "to the end" meant not just the end of the school but to the end of his life. In 1928, John Hallett Clark died just

The decline in Glenbow can be read in the Henderson Directory's statistics. In 1911, the population was 350; in 1914, it was fifty.

two years after his good neighbour Annie James's passing. The year before Mr. Clark's death, Currey and Betty Wearmouth, the last residents of Glenbow, had moved away to BC. Currey came back for Sarah Clark's auction and bought two gilt picture frames and a hammered silver bowl, which he and Betty always treasured.

That such a bright and varied bit of history as Glenbow's should come on with such force and then be gone so quickly and totally is an almost shocking thing—or maybe, simply instructive. Nothing much does last and the time interval taken to rise and fall may not, in the end, be the important thing. There is much to learn and think about at Glenbow, as much or more than many longer-lived places; and its quick flash allowed other things to be—such as Glenbow Ranch Provincial Park, which could not have existed had Chester de la Vergne got his bridge and his dream of a thriving, lasting town.

For those who know these stories, images will always swirl over the site of Glenbow, over Millionaire Hill and the quarry cliffs: a carload of stone reeling out of control, a high-spirited household maid dancing in her employer's fine dress, two children carrying a laundry basket up a steep hill—and maybe most poignant of all, the last houses of Glenbow skidding, horse-drawn, down the ice of the Bow River, on their way to a new address in Bowness.

The shacks of the town of Glenbow were one-by-one hauled away.

The Harvie Era

HOW A RIVER VALLEY GOES FROM BEING a town, quarry, and ranch to being a provincial park is an interesting and mysterious narrative—more interesting as you delve into it. It is not only the story of the valley but also that of a family: the Harvie family of Calgary and Cochrane.

When the town of Glenbow was no more, what remained was the de la Vergne ranch. In 1918, when the de la Vergnes moved into Calgary, Dick Widger was hired as ranch manager. In 1922, he leased the Glenbow Ranch and ran it until 1928. Widger was an Englishman, and, in imitation of his farming practice back in England, he once led his pigs from the Glenbow Ranch up the hill to the Morley Trail and down to the rail yards at Cochrane.

When Mr. Widger left, three Mennonite families took over, two living in the de la Vergne house and the third in the Moore house. Next to manage the Glenbow Ranch was the William Scott family from Ireland, beginning in 1931. Their arrangement with Chester de la Vergne was to run the ranch on a share basis. As will be seen, the Scotts would remain part of the Glenbow Ranch saga for generations.

The "millionaire" mansions that stood along the borders of Glenbow Ranch were either rented or stood vacant in the years after the town's demise. In 1928, Dr. Morris and his son, Dudley Jr., returned to Glenbow and found, to their sadness, that their old summer home had been vandalized. It was their last visit.

The nearby Drake house on Buckspring Ranch went through several hands. Major Condie Landale, of the *other* Glenbow Ranch downriver from de la Vergne's Glenbow Ranch, lived on the Buckspring from 1926 to 1928. After that, the well-known explorer R.M. Patterson purchased the ranch. Patterson had just completed his explorations of Yukon's Nahanni River, and, during his four years at the Buckspring, he used the ranch as a base of operations for explorations of the upper Highwood, the Highwood Pass, and Kananaskis Lakes.

Eric Lafferty Harvie as a young Lieutenant in World War I: 49th Battalion, Edmonton Regiment.

In 1934, the Buckspring Ranch was sold to Calgary lawyer, R.C. Burns.

The Stevenson house remained empty and deteriorated steadily.

The Wall Street crash of 1929 was particularly hard on those who'd had surplus money to invest during the Roaring Twenties. Chester de la Vergne was a typical case. After his hopes for Glenbow failed, he went into the car business in Calgary. He made other investments, such as in Alberta coal. When the Depression hit, his businesses failed and his investments plunged in value, a situation made worse by the fact that his two sisters in the United States had invested their funds in Chester's ventures. The entire family was in considerable trouble when Chester de la Vergne turned to his Calgary lawyer for help. That lawyer was Eric Lafferty Harvie. Born in Orillia, Ontario, in 1892, Eric Harvie had begun his legal education at Osgoode Hall, Toronto, and completed it at the University of Alberta in 1914. He articled in Calgary in the law offices of his uncle, James Short. A separate lure to Calgary was his uncle, Dr. James Lafferty, a Calgary doctor who had once been mayor of the city. By the time of his acquaintance with Chester de la Vergne, Eric Harvie was married to Dorothy Jean Southam of the Montreal Southam family. He was also a veteran of World War I, after serving in Europe with the 49th Battalion (Edmonton Regiment), in the 7th Canadian Infantry Brigade. He had been wounded by shrapnel during the trench warfare along the Somme River in 1916.

Ford, Miller, and Harvie had been retained by Chester de la Vergne, and Eric Harvie was de la Vergne's solicitor and council. Outside the law office, the Harvie family and the de la Vergne family became social friends. In 1925, Eric Harvie agreed to be president of Chester de la Vergne Company Ltd.

When the stock market crash of 1929 greatly reduced Chester de la Vergne's holdings, it was left to Eric Harvie to salvage what he could, particularly for the de la Vergne sisters. In his biography of E.L. Harvie, *A Gentleman from a Fading Age*, Fred M. Diehl went into considerable detail about how this was done. In brief, a new company, Glenbow Company Ltd., was created to take over the Chester de la Vergne Company's assets and liabilities in such a way that the more valuable assets were channelled to Chester's sisters. The liabilities associated with other assets stayed in Glenbow Company Ltd. Several letters from the de la Vergne family members express gratitude to Harvie for the way he handled their misfortune.

> The entire family was in considerable trouble when Chester de la Vergne turned to his Calgary lawyer for help. That lawyer was Eric Lafferty Harvie.

Eric Harvie (left) and Chester de la Vergne were fishing friends. Harvie was also de la Vergne's lawyer.

was still owned by Dr. Dudley Morris, though he had not been back since 1928. The house had been standing vacant, and, not surprisingly for the Depression era 1930s, squatters had moved in. That and the house's state of disrepair left Dorothy Harvie skeptical. She gave Eric a list of what would have to be done before she would consent to spend weekends there. Eric was not deterred. He contacted Dr. Morris, and, by 1938, the deal was done.

The Harvie family described their house and ranch at Glenbow as the "Sanctuary." Here, they went for walks and rides; fished, hunted, and otherwise observed and enjoyed nature. It became the place where Eric could get away from the increasing demands of his legal and business enterprises, while being within an hour's drive of the city. Essential to this was Dorothy Harvie's strict policing of the telephone. The people at Eric's office were allowed to phone only in the most dire of emergencies.

Important to the future of Glenbow Ranch, each of the Harvies' children had a relationship to the property that thickened with time. The three children were Margaret Joy, Donald Southam, and Frederick Neil Southam. Joy, the eldest, would in time go to McGill University, marry Don Maclaren, and raise a family in Quebec. She had been taught to love horses by her parents, and she brought her sons from Quebec to Glenbow Ranch as often as possible, so they would have a

In the end, ownership of the Glenbow Ranch shifted to Eric Harvie in 1934. Depression land prices were such that it was not worth a great deal in monetary terms but held promise as a recreational property for the Harvie family. The William Scott family continued to operate the ranch, much as they had done for Chester de la Vergne.

For the first couple of years of ownership, Eric and Dorothy Harvie had no house at Glenbow. They left their horses with the Scotts and came out on weekends to ride. Eric was on the lookout for a suitable weekend home and decided the best prospect was the Morris house. This

Eric Harvie with one of his prized hunting dogs, November 1948.

The old Morris house became E.L. and Dorothy Harvie's summer home at Glenbow.

other oil explorers, E.L. Harvie felt Alberta's real oil bonanza had yet to be found, and, in search of the big one, he participated in many promising ventures that came to naught.

The deal that would make Eric Harvie a solid fortune was the relatively quiet purchase of approximately five hundred thousand acres (202,342 hectares) of mineral rights near Edmonton. In western Canada, mineral rights are mostly owned by the Crown. Among the exceptions (where the mineral rights

strong connection to their grandparents and the ranch. Don Harvie remembered bringing friends to Glenbow Ranch, where they were under strict orders from Eric to do a morning's work before their leisure began. Neil's relationship to the ranch was different again; he loved horses and saw in the ranch a possible future for himself.

From his earliest days in Alberta, Eric Harvie had been interested in the province's oil industry. While still articling in his uncle's law office, Eric met the likes of W.S. Herron and Archibald Dingman, pioneers in the Turner Valley gas field. Before 1920, one of his legal clients was oil sands pioneer Alfred von Hammerstein, who was trying to find a commercial use for bitumen in the Fort McMurray area. In 1936, Eric was involved with the well that discovered oil under the gas cap on Turner Valley's west flank. Like many

Eric and Dorothy Harvie and their son Neil enjoy a summer afternoon at the "Sanctuary," 1945.

could be privately owned) were Canadian Pacific Railway land and Hudson's Bay Company land. The rights E.L. Harvie purchased in the Edmonton area (derisively known as the "Moose Pasture") were beneath former CPR land. The price of the mineral rights was modest because of a new provincial tax on mineral rights. The tax plus a lack of success by oil explorers in the region made the deal both available and affordable.

In 1947, after a string of dry holes, Imperial Oil hit a gusher at Leduc, Alberta. The strike was within Eric Harvie's "Moose Pasture." At the end of the 1940s, another even richer oil field was discovered at Redwater north of Edmonton, also within the boundaries of the Moose Pasture. In between the two strikes, E.L. Harvie's companies had shifted from leasing their land to other oil companies for option payments and royalties to hiring drilling rigs and taking the net proceeds themselves. The differ-ence in risk and potential profit was substantial, and, when Redwater proved to be an extremely rich oil field, Eric Harvie became a wealthy man: for a time the wealthiest from oil in Canada.

The story of Eric Harvie's financial success is interesting, but what he chose to do with his wealth is perhaps even more so. Before the dust had settled on the string of Alberta oil discoveries after Leduc, Eric Harvie had embarked on a campaign of philanthropy based on the principle that his money came from Alberta and Canada and, therefore, should return to the people of the prov-ince and nation. One of the expressions of his philanthropy was his choice to become a voracious collector of art,

E.L. Harvie, seen here on horseback by the Waverley Ranch house, came into possession of the Glenbow Ranch in 1934.

documents, and artefacts. These collections would, in time, become the basis of the impressive collection of the Glenbow Museum in Calgary. A statement that points toward his reasoning was that, while he himself could afford to travel the world and see its riches, 99 per cent of Canadians could not. He was bringing those riches home so all Canadians could share the experience.

He collected both outside and inside Canada. He acquired an early and brilliant selection of Canada's Inuit and West Coast First Nations Art. He collected art and artefacts related to Canada's history— so successfully that historians wishing to study especially western Canada's history make pilgrimage to the Glenbow Museum library and archives to this day.

Outside of Alberta, Eric Harvie– endowed foundations helped build the Confederation Arts Complex and Confederation Square in Charlottetown, Prince Edward Island. In Alberta, they played a powerful role in the growth and development of the Banff School of Fine

Arts (now The Banff Centre) and worthy projects to beautify communities across Alberta. The complete list of donations and projects based on Eric Harvie's wealth would require a book in itself.

The fact of Eric Harvie's philanthropy affects Glenbow Ranch Provincial Park in many ways, but the most important factor is the way public philanthropy became not just a feature of Eric Lafferty Harvie but of his entire family. The closeness of the Harvie family, and Eric and Dorothy's emphasis on family, made it possible for this principle of public generosity to pass forward into future generations.

But a chilling fact is that Glenbow Ranch Provincial Park came very close to not existing, for the simple and basic reason that it came close to not being Harvie property after 1946. That year, Eric Harvie sat down and wrote a letter that meticulously detailed the assets of Glenbow Ranch; a letter sent to a prospective buyer who had come forward to inquire if the property was for sale. That Eric Harvie used over five hundred words to write this description suggests strongly that he was willing to part with the ranch.

In Fred Diehl's biography of Eric Harvie, no explanation is given as to why the family's paradise in the country came so close to sale. The story ends with the cryptic line: "But the sale did not go through—and just as well."

"The Glenbow Ranch was indeed Eric's sanctuary. A place away from the madding crowd."

Ranching in the old-fashioned way: the early Neil Harvie years at Glenbow.

In closing his chapter on Eric Harvie's Sanctuary at Glenbow, Mr. Diehl writes: "The Glenbow Ranch was indeed Eric's sanctuary. A place away from the madding crowd. A place where he could ride with his family, enjoy his favourite meal of steak and kidney pie, hunt birds in season, train dogs and horses, practice skeet-shooting, or just sit on the hog's back that juts out into the valley below the house and commune with nature and sort out the intricacies of prevailing deals while surveying his domain."

Neil Southam Harvie, Eric and Dorothy's youngest son, is said to have been interested in ranching from the age of twelve. He loved horses and spent many of his weekends and portions of his summers riding at Glenbow Ranch. By the time Neil finished high school, he knew that he wanted a future in agriculture. He enrolled in Alberta's Vermilion School of Agriculture for a year (which he considered his best year of schooling) then transferred to the University of Alberta. He graduated in Agriculture from U of A in 1953.

Neil Harvie in 1946. He would choose to make ranching at Glenbow his career.

In the same time period, E.L. Harvie purchased the Bearspaw Ranch, the historic ranch that was immediately downstream from the Glenbow Ranch. But later, when a deal was struck to run the Bearspaw Ranch, it was between Neil Harvie and ranch manager, Wilf Carr.

During the summers and holidays of Neil's years at the University of Alberta, he worked at the Bearspaw Ranch with Wilf Carr and lived in the old Bearspaw ranch house.

In 1954, Neil Harvie and Robin Williams were married. Robin had grown up in Calgary, where her father and grandfather were partners in an accounting firm. The Williams family lived just three blocks away from the Harvies' Calgary home in Elbow Park, but Neil and Robin were not properly acquainted until they were both attending the University of Alberta, Robin in Commerce and Neil in Agriculture. They were matched up on a double date by one of Neil's fraternity friends.

On completion of her BCom in 1953, Robin returned to Calgary and worked

Rancher David
Scott, 2007

Robin Harvie (Neil's wife, and mother of Pauli, Tim, Carol, and Katie) on a cattle drive in 1958. The photo was taken in what is now Glenbow Ranch Provincial Park.

On the Glenbow Ranch hill where Eric Harvie liked to sit and watch and think, the family erected this monument.

full time for her family's accounting firm. After she and Neil were married, it was off to Bearspaw Ranch and life in the old Landale ranch house. They did have electricity, albeit thirty-two volt (glass batteries in the garage). Refrigeration was achieved with ice from the Alberta Ice Company, where they also rented a meat locker.

Robin's early experiences on the ranch included running a horse-drawn rake in haying time, feeding a litter of orphaned piglets in a box behind the stove, chasing cattle on horseback, and taking long rides with Neil on the best of summer nights.

Tale of Two Glenbow Ranches

For a time, two Glenbow Ranches existed. The name Glenbow (shortened from Glen on the Bow) seems to have originated with Canadian Pacific Railway. Glenbow Station first appeared on the CPR timetable in 1889, though the station existed prior to this. In the January 21, 1905, *Calgary Herald*, the Local and General column stated that "Mrs. F. Houghton of the Glenbow Ranche went west last night." It is assumed they meant west by train. The property the Houghtons owned was section 23 of township 25 (range 3, west of the 4th meridian), adjacent to and immediately downstream from what would become the de la Vergne's Glenbow Ranch in 1909. Houghton's Glenbow Ranche contained the CPR station called Bearspaw, but the ranch was still known as the Glenbow when it was sold to Edward Guy Warner in November 1906; and it was still Glenbow Ranch when Warner decided to sell it and move to the West Coast in 1907. Perhaps unable to sell the property at this time, Mr. Warner leased it to Edward Payn le Sueur for five years. According to Alberta Land Titles, William Parslow bought section 23 on March 27, 1911, and sold it the same day to Alfred Crewdson, who leased it back to Parslow. Major A.C. (Condie) Landale, a British army officer and avid polo player, was Alfred Crewdson's first cousin, and the Condie Landale family lived at the ranch house for several years.

In the 1930s, the ranch's ownership passed to the Sykes family of Calgary, who would sell it to E.L. Harvie in 1949. By this time, the ranch was definitely called the Bearspaw Ranch.

The Scott Family

L to R: Lorne Umbach, Sam Scott, Heather Scott (Sam's daughter), Adelaide Scott (Sam's mother), c. 1946.

The Scott family's ties to the Glenbow Ranch started in 1928 when William Scott made an arrangement with Chester de la Vergne to run the ranch on shares. The Scotts came from County Down in Northern Ireland. William and his son Sam came first in 1923 and worked on the construction of railway tracks and irrigation ditches. They returned to Ireland for several years before returning to Alberta with the rest of the Scott family in 1929. In Ireland, William had trained horses, both to ride and to show. He was famous at Glenbow for his dogs. He could stand on the hill where the Scotts lived in the manager's house and direct his dogs to herd the cattle by hand signals.

In 1934, Eric Harvie took over ownership of the Glenbow Ranch, and the Scotts stayed on. William Scott and his wife retired from the ranch and moved to Cochrane in 1957. Sam Scott and his wife Helen took over. Helen was born in Calgary and had followed in her mother's footsteps to become a one-room school teacher, first at Hussar and then at Glendale, north of Glenbow. Sam Scott invited the young school teacher to go riding with him, and they were married in 1935. In 1939, Helen was a founder of the Glendale Women's Institute, which Robin Harvie joined and to which Robin still proudly belongs.

Sam Scott was in the air force for the duration of World War II but returned to Glenbow Ranch afterward. He was active in the Calgary Stampede: in the wild horse race and as an outrider in the chuckwagon races. He also trained horses and showed them at the Calgary Horse Show. He continued to feed his cattle with a horse team and hayrack until 1970, when he and Helen retired from the Glenbow Ranch and moved to Cochrane. David Scott continued his family's involvement in the Glenbow Ranch, and his father's involvement in outriding for chuckwagon races. His present-day farm borders Glenbow Ranch Provincial Park.

Neil Harvie weighing cattle on a feedlot scale originally used at the Glenbow rail station.

Neil acquired his pilot's licence in the early 1960s. He purchased a Piper Super Cub and used it to supervise the growing ranch: checking fences, waterers, gates, and cattle.

At this stage, both the Scotts on Glenbow Ranch and Neil and Wilf Carr on the Bearspaw were still haying with horses.

These years of proving himself on the Bearspaw Ranch led to Neil Harvie's taking over all the Harvie ranching interests at Glenbow. Over the coming years, the Bearspaw Ranch and other local acquisitions were added to Glenbow Ranches Ltd. until the total acreage rose above twelve thousand acres.

Neil and Robin Harvie's first child, a daughter, Pauli, was born in late 1955. Soon after, the family moved into their newly built home on the north hill. Three more children would follow: Tim (1957), Carol (1959), and Katie (1962).

Neil and Robin Harvie's era at Glenbow Ranches Ltd. was one of selective modernization. East and west of Glenbow Ranch Provincial Park, also across the Bow, portions of land were farmed and an irrigation system instituted. Neil acquired his pilot's licence in the early 1960s. He purchased a Piper Super Cub and used it to supervise the growing ranch: checking fences, waterers, gates, and cattle. Robin Harvie also earned a flying licence and flew the Cub during the '60s. The plane remains in the family and is still an important tool on the ranch; Tim Harvie flies it in the present day, for the same purpose of keeping track of the ranch.

At the same time, horses have never gone out of use on Glenbow Ranch.

Another example of old and new that existed in the Neil and Robin Harvie period was the weigh scale that was once part of the facilities at Glenbow Station, which Neil moved across the river flat to be part of his feedlot operation. Robin Harvie says, "You have no idea how many thousands of cattle we weighed on that old scale."

As a rancher, Neil Harvie stood for both innovation and conservation. On the innovation side, he was one of eight founders of a beef cattle initiative called Beefbooster. One of the founders, John Stewart-Smith, describes the principle of Beefbooster this way: "Our firm belief [was] that hybrid bulls are ultimately superior to purebred bulls, because of the ability to pick and choose to get the best of any breed in the offspring."

This was obviously a challenge to the centuries-old reliance on purebred cattle to effect herd improvement. Beefbooster sought to replace the old methods with hybridization of superior individual cattle, as identified by science and intense bookkeeping on the ranch. The results achieved by Beefbooster operations were compelling, and the ideas are still powerful within the ranching industry.

On the conservation side, Neil Harvie sought to conserve the virtues of "prairie wool," Canada's native prairie grass, whose incredible species complexity allows it to survive extremes of climate.

Foothills Fescue Research Institute

Grassland ecosystems retain and filter water, produce rich forage for wildlife, and remove carbon from the atmosphere and sequester it naturally. In appreciation of the amazing abilities and complexities of native grassland, the Glenbow Ranch Park Foundation established the Foothills Fescue Research Institute (FFRI) in 2009, with the mission of becoming "a World Centre of Excellence for the Study of Western North American Native Grassland Species."

The institute studies native plant species and is establishing effective means by which the park, private industry, and individuals can work together to conserve and restore grassland biodiversity and functionality.

FFRI is also pursuing a more in-depth understanding of invasive plant species: how to control weeds and prevent the loss of grassland to competitive, non-native plants.

In some areas of Glenbow Ranch Provincial Park where the soils have been disturbed, nature is able to reclaim the bare land with native species. But in other situations, the invasive species take hold and outcompete the plants originally there.

Glenbow Ranch Provincial Park presents institute researchers with the opportunity to carry out long-term studies on native grassland, to work with nature from the ground up.

Neil Harvie's reasoning was that a great deal of ecologically sensitive land all across Canada could be preserved through donation if the government offered tax receipts equivalent to the value of the gift.

In the western fringe of the Great Plains, Glenbow Ranch Provincial Park's region, where the prairie rises through foothills to meet the Rocky Mountains, native grass is visually dominated by tussocks of the fescue grass species. Neil lent his assistance and backing to several initiatives devoted to the preservation of fescue grassland, and one of the goals of Glenbow Ranch Provincial Park is to be a laboratory and seed source toward saving this threatened landscape and the plant species it supports.

Larry Simpson, the first employee of the Nature Conservancy of Canada, was a close friend to Neil Harvie. Robin Harvie remembers the two having long discussions about how native prairie and other threatened landscapes of Canada could be protected and sustained. Simpson hoped to convince Harvie to allow Nature Conservancy caveats to be placed on the Glenbow Ranch titles, but Neil resisted, mainly because he believed a change to Canada's charitable donation rules could effect even more comprehensive protection. Driving Neil was a determination to keep his ranch from falling into the hands of developers: becoming yet more suburbs and exurbs of the rapidly growing city of Calgary.

When the decisions were made regarding donation of Glenbow Ranch land toward the creation of Glenbow Ranch Provincial Park, Neil Harvie was gone; he died in 1999. The decisions were made by the new owners: his four children. However, Neil Harvie had done something that greatly aided his children in their historic bequest. Neil had met with government and also funded research into the tax rules governing donations of land. Neil's reasoning was that a great deal of ecologically sensitive land all across Canada could be preserved through donation if the government offered tax receipts equivalent to the value of the gift—as in fact the government had been doing with other kinds of donations, such as works of art.

Ultimately, the strength of this argument prevailed. In 1995, Environment Canada created the Ecological Gifts Program, containing the very changes to the Income Tax Act that Neil Harvie had sought. In 2006, the federal government removed capital gains tax from these donations, and the program became even more attractive. Since 1995, there have been over $500 million worth of ecological gifts to Canada. One of these, of course, was the 2006 Harvie family's offer to sell their land at about 60 per cent of the market value to the Government of Alberta, which allowed 1,304 hectares (3,246 acres) of the Glenbow Ranch to be designated Glenbow Ranch Provincial Park.

Based on an appraisal of $67 million, the Government of Alberta paid the family $40 million, accompanied by a

$27 million tax receipt. (A more recent appraisal of the land put the value over $80 million.) Further, the Harvies provided $6 million to a newly created Harvie Conservancy Foundation, the money to be divided between development of Glenbow Ranch Provincial Park and of the Lois Hole Centennial Provincial Park near conservationist Lois Hole's home of St. Albert, Alberta.

In his speech on behalf of the family at the announcement of the agreement, on August 23, 2006, Tim Harvie admitted that at times, since the family's decision, he would look across the Bow River from his home at the lovely portion of valley where he had grown up, and which he and his siblings were now giving up, and wonder about the decision.

In June 2010, the Nature Conservancy of Canada awarded the Harvie family their highest Alberta honour: the Alberta Order of Conservation, the first time the honour was bestowed.

After Eric L. Harvie's death in 1975, Eric and Dorothy's sanctuary, their summer home at Glenbow Ranch, stood vacant, sometimes for lengthy periods. On a winter morning in 1977, Neil Harvie got a call at the ranch telling him that the old house was on fire. The fire department had been called, but by the time help arrived, there was little left but the two fireplaces. The firemen were wetting down the outbuildings, and one of them asked Neil if they should try to protect the outhouse that was quite near the blaze. At first Neil said not to bother, then he changed his mind. He flung open the outhouse door, and two children were there, cowering. In time, the two frightened children were able to tell their story. They had run away from home in Cochrane, travelling along the CPR right-of-way. They saw the Harvie house, climbed the hill to it, and gained entrance through the coal chute. They made themselves a fire in one of the fireplaces. They found some blankets, pulled a chesterfield close, and went to sleep—but they had forgotten to put the screen back in front of the fire. A cinder caught the chesterfield on fire. The children woke up and managed to escape, concealing themselves in the outhouse as a last resort.

None of the house's contents were saved; a great many personal mementos were lost. At the time, Dorothy Harvie and Robin Harvie were holidaying together in California. When Dorothy Harvie received the news that the old Glenbow summer house was gone, she said, "Well perhaps that is as it should be—the end of an era."

"Well perhaps that is as it should be— the end of an era."

The Legacy

THIS BOOK COMMEMORATES GLENBOW Ranch Provincial Park's official opening: the occasion on which the people of Alberta received this amazing legacy from the group Tim Harvie calls "The Big Four." This is a smiling reference to the group of four ranchers who donated the funds needed for the first ever Calgary Stampede in 1912. The Big Four of Glenbow Ranch Provincial Park are Pauli Smith, Tim Harvie, Carol Raymond, and Katie Harvie, who have followed their own wishes and those of their father, Neil Harvie, and their mother, Robin Harvie, in parting with this amazing place, so that others will be able to enjoy it, now and in the future.

In most reputable dictionaries, the word "legacy" means simply a gift or bequest, but there is a connotation of the word that suggests something much larger. For example, when we look at a long-serving political leader who has signalled a desire to retire, there are usually a few final pieces of legislation meant as his or her legacy: gifts to the nation that represent what that leader was all about. So legacy can be more than a gift given on a birthday or at Christmas. Legacy, in certain cases, can be a significant gift or bequest that contains within it important messages, directions, symbolism, and, perhaps, the distilled meaning of the lives of the people behind the gift.

In the case of the Harvie family and Glenbow Ranch Provincial Park, a family with a rare set of attributes, honed over several generations, has provided a valuable legacy to the province and the nation, while also providing an example of philanthropy to those with the means to be donors. There are messages here for everyone.

Eric Harvie believed that he owed a debt to the place that had given him a good life and the opportunity to prosper. As an oilman, his wealth came from the

The decision to carry out Neil Harvie's dream of a park was left to his and Robin Harvie's children, the group Tim Harvie calls "The Big Four." L to R: Carol Raymond, Pauli Smith, Tim Harvie, and Katie Harvie.

land, the geological horizons underlying it, and he sought in the last half of his life to give back to the land a considerable portion of what he had earned from it. His "joke" was that he planned to die broke, and the flurry of bequests before and immediately after his death, through the various foundations he endowed, certainly reduced his personal worth dramatically. He passed on these unusual and potent ideas to his close-knit family, along with a powerful mixture of values that highlighted responsibility, discipline, activity, and fun—also a love of landscape and animals. That recipe was powerfully

ingested by his children and then passed along to their own children. At the current end of that line we find Glenbow Ranch Provincial Park. A legacy.

Another aspect of the Harvie family legacy is the example set for other Albertans who have achieved wealth directly or indirectly from the province's oil and gas economy. To test the proposition that the Harvie example has had impact, I asked a wealthy Alberta oilman, who happened also to have a penchant for collecting and housing important artefacts and documents, what Eric Harvie meant to him. He said he felt

Right: Eric Harvie surveys the valley from horseback.

that Eric Harvie had provided an example of how economically powerful Albertans could deal with the opportunities wealth created. Had Eric Harvie influenced him, I asked. Yes, he had.

Still another way that legacy works in the Harvie example is how Neil Harvie sought to change the tax rules that governed donations of land. He expressed the wish to his children that land from the Glenbow Ranch be preserved in a park; but he went further. By arguing success-fully for tax receipts for donated land that were equivalent to the tax incentive for other kinds of donations, he bestowed a legacy that has rippled outward across the entire nation, such that thousands and thousands of hectares of ecologically significant land have been preserved that likely would not have been without the tax rule changes. The rippling effect of his arguments and his funding of research into these tax matters have continued to create changes. Eleven years after the first legal shift (donation tax receipts for land), the federal government eliminated capital gains tax from the Ecological Gifts Program, thus removing another obstacle and creating potential for a further flood of important land donations.

Now that Glenbow Ranch Provincial Park exists, and is open to the public, the responsibilities of legacy pass to the rest of us: the people of Alberta, of Canada; even to the people of other countries who visit here. Each visitor, while enjoying and learning from the park, will be responsible for the heritage grass that grows beside each pathway, for the native wildflowers that bloom in that grass. For all the flora and fauna that live here, and for all the archaeological traces of life that went before, we are now responsible.

Levity and weight. Fun and discipline. An important and beautiful space allowed to resist the mantra of development so that something older can meet the future in peace.

"*To all future visitors to Glenbow Ranch Provincial Park, my wish is this: that you feast your mind and senses, and enjoy.*"

Tim Harvie

Selected Sources and Further Reading

Introduction and Bow River

Armstrong, Christopher, Matthew Evenden, and H.V. Nelles. *The River Returns: An Environmental History of the Bow*. McGill University Press, 2009.

First Nations on the Bow

McMillan, Alan D, and Eldon Yellowhorn. *First Peoples in Canada*. D&M Publishers Inc., Vancouver, 2004.

Two Worlds Meet

Dempsey, Hugh. *Firewater: The Impact of the Whisky Trade on the Blackfoot Nation*. Fifth House Publishers, Calgary, 2002.

Silversides, Brock. *Fort de Prairie: The Story of Fort Edmonton*. Heritage House Publishing Co., Vancouver, 2005.

Stenson, Fred. *The Trade* (novel). D & M Publishers Inc., Vancouver, 2000.

Thompson, David (edited by Barbara Belyea). *Columbia Journals*. McGill University Press, 1994.

The Cochrane Ranche

Classen, Henry C. *Eye on the Future: Business People in Calgary and the Bow Valley—1870–1900*. University of Calgary Press, Calgary, 2002.

Elofson, Warren M. *Cowboys, Gentlemen and Cattle Thieves: Ranching on the Western Frontier*. McGill University Press, 2000.

Evans, Simon M. *The Bar U and Canadian Ranching History*. University of Calgary Press, Calgary, 2004.

Stenson, Fred. *Lightning* (novel). D&M Publishers Inc., Vancouver, 2003.

Millionaire Hill and Glenbow Village

Glendale Women's Institute, *Taming the Prairie Wood: A History of the Districts of Glendale, Westminster and Bearspaw, West of Calgary*.

Read, Tracey. *Acres and Empires: A History of the Municipal District of Rocky View No. 44*, 1983.

Cochrane and Area Historical Society. *Big Hill Country: Cochrane and Area*, 1977.

The Harvie Era and The Legacy

Cochrane Historical and Archival Preservation Society. *More Big Hill Country: Cochrane and Area, 1945–1980; 2009*.

Diehl, Fred. *A Gentleman from a Fading Age: Eric Lafferty Harvie*, 1989.

Image Credits

Front cover: Patrick Price

Back cover and front flap: Heather Simonds

Page i: Ken Wright

Page 1: Heather Simonds

Page 2: Patrick Price (top), Heather Simonds (left)

Page 3: Ken Wright

Page 4: Ken Wright (bottom left), Glenbow Ranch Park Foundation (top right), Patrick Price (bottom right)

Page 5: Map by Kim Koons, with modifications by John Luckhurst

Page 6: Glenbow Ranch Park Foundation (map), photo credits listed elsewhere on this page

Page 7: Heather Simonds, Glenbow Ranch Park Foundation (background image)

Page 8: Michael Interisano

Page 9: Heather Simonds

Page 10: Heather Simonds

Page 11: Urban Systems Ltd. (top), Heather Simonds (bottom)

Page 12: Alberta Culture and Community Spirit, Historic Resources Management (top); Glenbow Ranch Park Foundation (two photos, right); Heather Simonds (bottom left)

Page 13: Heather Simonds

Page 14: Heather Simonds (top and bottom)

Page 15: Patrick Price

Page 16: Heather Simonds (left), Carl Buell (illustration)

Page 17: Glenbow Ranch Park Foundation

Page 18: Glenbow Archives NA-5217-1

Page 19: iStock

Page 20: Heather Simonds (left), Alberta Culture and Community Spirit (right)

Page 21: Bison Effigy, Northern Plains, c. 1200, green quartzite, Collection of Glenbow Museum, Calgary, Canada, AX 70 (left), Heather Simonds (right)

Pages 22 and 23: Glenbow Archives NA-249-78, Heather Simonds (background rocks image)

Page 24: Paul Kane, Assiniboine Hunting Buffalo, c. 1851-1856, Paul Kane, National Gallery of Canada, Ottawa

Page 24 and 25: Glenbow Archives NA-1700-156

Page 26: Glenbow Archives PD-87-11-14 (left), Ivan Kocsis (right bottom)

Page 27: Royal Saskatchewan Museum 94-254-16

Page 28: Glenbow Archives NA-395-14

Page 29: Glenbow Archives B199-B2

Page 30: Raw Eater's Story Robe, early 20th century, moosehide and paint, Collection of Glenbow Museum, Calgary, Canada, AF 870 (left), National Gallery of Canada, C.W. Jefferys, Library and Archives Canada 1972-26-1406 (right)

Page 31: Artist H.P. Share, Engraver J.W. Evans, Picturesque Canada, Vol. I, 1882 (top right), Glenbow Archives PB-885-10 (bottom)

Page 32: 952.169.1: Blackfoot Indian Encampment, Foothills of the Rocky Mountains (watercolour over pencil, touches of gouache, pen and ink?), date unknown, Armstrong, William; ROM2006_7731_1; 8.5 x 11, 300 dpi, TIF, PC, via FTP

Page 33: Paul Kane, Canadian (1810-1871), Fort Edmonton, 1846, watercolor and pencil on paper, 5 1/2 x 9 inches, Stark Museum of Art, Orange, Texas, 31.78.133

Page 35: Glenbow Archives NA-659-43

Page 36: D.B. Robinson, "Crowfoot - Blood Chief," no date, watercolour on paper, Collection of Glenbow Museum, Calgary, Canada, 59.61.1

Page 37: Oliver B. Buell, CPR Archives, A.4188 (right); Richard Barrington Nevitt, "Fort Calgary in Summer," c. 1876, watercolour on paper, Collection of Glenbow Museum, Calgary, Canada, 74.7.53 (bottom)

Page 38: Glenbow Archives NA-626-1 (left), Heather Simonds (background rocks image), Glenbow Ranch Park Foundation (background grass image)

Page 39: Glenbow Archives NA-127-1 (top), Heather Simonds (bottom)

Page 40: Glenbow Archives NA-102-21

Page 41: Heather Simonds

Page 42: Heather Simonds

Page 43: Glenbow Archives NA-239-25 (top left), Glenbow Archives NA 237-7 (right), Heather Simonds (background rocks image)

Page 44: Heather Simonds (left), Patrick Price (right)

Page 45: McCord Museum 11-109-119

Page 46 Karol Dabbs (bottom), Heather Simonds (background rocks image)

Page 47: Glenbow Archives PA-368-71 (top), Glenbow Archives S-222-58 (bottom)

Page 48: Copyright expired, accessed at Wikipedia.com (left), Glenbow Ranch Park Foundation (background images)

Page 49: Glenbow Archives S-222-58, (left), Glenbow Archives S-222-200

Page 50: Heather Simonds (top right and top left)

Page 51: Glenbow Archives NA-239-13

Page 52: Heather Simonds (front and background)

Page 53: Heather Simonds

Page 54: Glenbow Archives NA-1697-1 (left), Heather Simonds (background rocks image), Glenbow Ranch Park Foundation (background grass image)

Page 55: Heather Simonds

Page 56: Cockbaine family archives

Page 57: Cockbaine family archives

Page 58: Cockbaine family archives (top left), Glenbow Archives NA-1080-2

Page 59: Ken Wright (right and bottom)

Page 60: Glenbow Archives NA-644-9

Page 61: Malvern College Archives (top left), Glenbow Archives NA-1058-3

Page 62: Glenbow Archives PA-3689-108

Page 63: Kennerley family archives, Glenbow Ranch Park Foundation (background)

Page 64: Kennerley family archives

Page 65: Heather Simonds

Page 66: Glenbow Ranch Park Foundation

Page 67: Glenbow Archives NA-1042-11

Page 68: Gillespie family archives

Page 69: Glenbow Archives NA-1025-2

Page 70: Glenbow Archives NA-1025-1, Glenbow Ranch Park Foundation (background grass image), Heather Simonds (background rocks image)

Page 71: Glenbow Archives PA-3641-2 (right), Heather Simonds (background image)

Page 72: Glenbow Archives NA-1092-2

Page 73: Harvie family archives

Page 74: Kennerley family archives (top), Heather Simonds (bottom)

Page 75: Glenbow Archives NA-1092-3

Page 76: Sinclair Stevenson family archives (left), Glenbow Archives NA-1061-3 (top right), Heather Simonds (bottom right), Glenbow Ranch Park Foundation (background)

Page 77: Morris family archives

Page 78: Canadian Aviation and Space Museum CASM-3091 (top left), Smith College Archive (top right), Glenbow Archives NA-3956-1 (bottom left)

Page 78 and 79: Glenbow Archives NA-156-8, Heather Simonds (background rocks image)

Page 80: Heather Simonds

Page 81: Glenbow Archives NA-962-5 (top), Glenbow Archives NA-1092-7 (bottom)

Page 82: Heather Simonds

Page 83: Glenbow Archives NA-962-6

Page 84: Ken Wright

Page 85: Harvie family archives

Page 86: Glenbow Archives NA-1127 (left), Heather Simonds (right)

Page 87: Glenbow Archives NA-1061-16

Page 88: Patrick Price

Page 89: Heather Simonds

Page 90: Glenbow Archives G1-1204-1a

Page 91: Glenbow Archives NB-17-29 (top left), Heather Simonds (top right), Harvie family archives (bottom right)

Page 92: Harvie family archives (top and bottom)

Page 93: Harvie family archives

Page 94: Heather Simonds

Page 95: Roy Farran, North Hill News, Harvie family archives (top), Harvie family archives (bottom)

Page 96: Patrick Price

Page 97: Roy Farran, North Hill News, Harvie family archives (top left), Patrick Price (bottom left), Glenbow Ranch Park Foundation (background grass image), Heather Simonds (background rocks image)

Page 98: Scott family archives, Glenbow Ranch Park Foundation (background grass image), Heather Simonds (background rock image)

Page 99: Heather Simonds

Page 100: Harvie family archives

Page 101: Heather Simonds (left and background rock image), Glenbow Ranch Park Foundation (background grass image)

Page 102: Heather Simonds

Page 103: Heather Simonds

Page 104: Heather Simonds

Page 105: Patrick Price

Page 106: Heather Simonds

Page 107: Heather Simonds

Page 108: Calgary Herald (top), Heather Simonds (left)

Page 109: Harvie family archives

Page 110: Heather Simonds

Page 111: Patrick Price (left), Heather Simonds (right)

Page 112 and 113: Heather Simonds

Author photo: Greg Gerrard

Index